A NORTH WESTMORELAND VILLAGE LAD

Robinson Wharton

Wilton Publishing Co. 1999

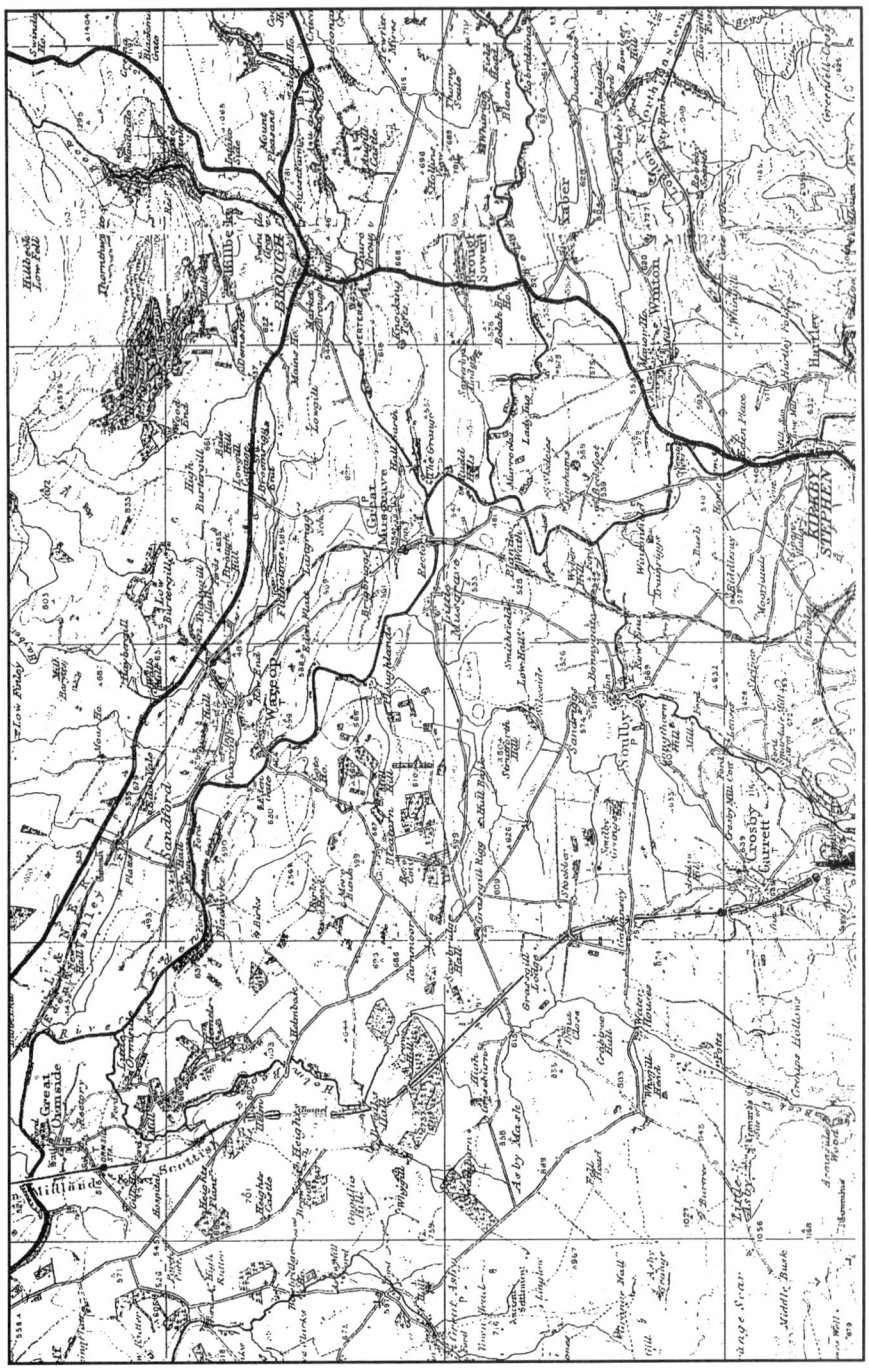

A North Westmoreland Village Lad
by Robinson Wharton
ISBN 0 9536131 0 0
First Published 1999

Copyright © Malcolm and Ian Wharton 1999
Robinson Wharton has asserted his right under the Copyright,
Designs and Patents Act 1988 to be identified as the author of this work.

All rights reserved. No part of this publication may be reproduced, stored in a retrieval system, or transmitted in any form or by any means, electronic, mechanical, photocopying, recording or otherwise without the prior permission of the publisher.

Published in the UK by Wilton Publishing Co.
Hartpury House, Hartpury, Gloucester GL19 3BE

Printed by Cerberus Printing
Kirkby Stephen, Cumbria CA17 4QD

ABOUT THE AUTHOR

Robinson Wharton was born at Winton, the eldest son of a family of four children the other children were two elder sisters Evie, and Hilda and a younger brother Ivan.

Robinson attended the village school at Winton from the age of 5 to 13 years before leaving to start work on local farms. He has lived and worked with farmers in Cumberland, Westmoreland and Lancashire all his working life, except for 4 years 1942 - 1946 army service.

He is now retired and resides at Morland with his wife Mary.

**Grateful thanks to the following people
who provided photographs**

Mr A. Allan, Mrs E. Bell, Mr E. Coulthard,
Mrs Mary Coulthard, Mrs E. Coward,
Mrs E. Dent, Mr M. Gregson, Mr J.A. Harris,
Mrs J. Lord and Mr J.B. Marston

Preface

This book transcribes memories of life in the 30s, as seen by a village lad just written as remembered. I apologise but not in a precise order. Mainly of Winton, Hartley, Kirkby Stephen and North Westmoreland.

Agriculture was the prime industry in the village and therefore the book focuses on the farming methods at the time, the interdependence of most of the village population on agriculture, and the ancillary industries supporting it, and part history and customs of the area.

My life during the period covered by the book was one that involved school and farming and I hope that the book will give you an interesting insight into life in a rural Westmoreland village.

Winton has changed in many ways since the 1930's. In those days there were two chapels, two shops, a public house and a school and 51 dwellings. Today there is one chapel, one public house and a village hall and getting near 100 dwellings. The village hall is now very much the hub of village life and is in constant need of funds for maintenance, running expenses, and indeed long-term capital improvements.

I feel that the ongoing viability of the village hall is critical to the life of Winton and I am donating £1 from each First Edition book that is sold.

Looking back now that I am retired, I think of the times and days when I was aged from 7 to 18 years, 1931-1942; what things were like and how everyone lived, how things are today in 1999, and by writing it down, I thought it would be of interest to those who are interested in bygone days.

I was born at Winton (one mile out of Kirkby Stephen) with one brother and two sisters. I attended Winton school, which in those days had on average 52 pupils. The Head teacher was Miss Kent and her assistant Miss Akrigg. They both used to cycle daily from Kirkby Stephen. The first 18 years of my life rotated around this area.

Agriculture was the number one industry. Nearly everyone who lived in the area was associated with it, or had been at some times in their lives. My first real encounter with farming was going down 50 yards to the nearest farm to help the farmer/dealer, Anthony Allan, who took me under his wing. Nearly every night after school and weekends I was there, either helping out on the farm or going with him on his visits to other farms, dealing.

Now, to picture the farmer/dealer; his farm was not that big. But Anthony was a very astute dealer, businessman, and stockman. However he was reluctant to change his ways. The old fashioned ways and systems were still good enough for him. It was a case of making do and mend. He had bits of land rented within a 5 mile radius. Permanent stock would be say 8 cows, young replacement stock, bullocks and 50 fell ewes, 1 work horse, 2 breeding mares which were nearly always on the fell. The main weekly income would be butter made and sold, and eggs, and dealing. His main dealing was in new calved cattle which he bought locally direct off the farms and at Kirkby Stephen auction on the Monday. His main market for selling was Hellifield auction on the Thursday, where all the town dairy cow keepers from Leeds, Bradford, Silsden and the other industrial towns, came weekly for their replacements. The cattle all having been sent by rail on the Wednesday evening from the top station at Kirkby Stephen. His other outlet was to farmers who were in the new business of producing milk for the new outlet for whole milk at Express Dairies, Appleby, for the London trade. Another main line of his was buying cows in calf, mostly in the summer to graze these bits of land he had, then selling them when calved. Plus he did quite a bit of trade in rearing calves and stags; also, like every other farmer, he reared 4 - 6 bullocks yearly. He lived at Hill House with the Father, Ned, his Mother and Uncle Jim, and after he lost his father and mother, he married Ada Robley, and they later adopted Frankie, Frankie being Ada's great-nephew. Many was the time I had Frankie on my knee and gave him his pobs.

Calf Dealing

As I stated earlier, Anthony Allan used to do a bit of calf dealing, and his main time of year was May/June when most cows calved down. This ensured we made the most use of the summer grass. He always had 2 or 3 of his own calving down, plus there were surplus calves in the village or round about to be bought and he would get 6 or 7 together, mostly bull calves, roaned if possible, but other colours with the price appertaining to colour. Then out came the rear seat of his car and we loaded them up loose, no bags involved, as at each call they were all inspected. Perhaps 2 loads into Swaledale, 1 South Stainmore, 1 North Stainmore, 1 Brough/Musgrave, and 1 Fell End, and part loads here and there to order.

It had to be a good backed roan bull calf for £1. If it had the potential for a breeding bull, and a hearsay pedigree - 30 bob. But Anthony Allan's limit was the pound or guinea mark. No more than say £6 in a full car load and with 1 at this call, perhaps 2 at another, we always managed to sell out. Not a fortune made, but a service given.

I always remember taking 3 calves to Tin Bridge Farm between Great Musgrave and Brough which is no longer a farm and on arrival the farmer set off, 'I haven't ordered any calves!'. Anthony Allen said, 'Oh yes you did. It was in the auction about 6 weeks ago.' 'Well, I have nowhere to put them.' Anthony Allan said, 'There must be somwhere.' Just then his wife appeared. His wife had a good look at the 3 calves and said, 'They and me will have to find somewhere. We have got to have summat to rear.' Well, the farmer said, 'Reet, the only spot doing nowt is the sitting room. It's empty. Will thou have em in there?' And that is where we put them! The only other incident re this trip, the farmer's wife said, 'Come in and have some coffee.' And were them squares tough. Nowt but flour and watter. No milk or lard had been used in baking them!

All the cattle in our area were Shorthorns, except every Spring Thompsons of Stobars Hall, J and M Coward of Winton Manor and D Burrell of Winton went to the Sands, Carlisle, where the Irish brought in boatloads of feeding cattle. Mostly black bullocks and heifers which they summer grazed to sell fat, or sell at the Luke Fair Sales. Of the Shorthorns, the heifers were reared and generally calved down twice, the milk being used for butter making and calf rearing and then sold after the third calf, when at their peak, to go into the town dairies cow keepers for milk production: Bradford, Leeds, Liverpool, etc. However, now there was the new producer with Flying Herds starting to supply Express Dairies at Appleby. Every Monday Kirkby Stephen Auction would have 25 - 30 newly calved cows and heifers, and the dealers would be local dealers buying for sale again to the town dairies at Hellifield or Haslingden. Dealers also came from the Hellifield area, Clitheroe, Bishop Auckland, Durham, Appleby and Penrith. The Hellifield dealers would also buy at Middleton in Teesdale on the Tuesday and Barnard Castle on the Wednesday, therefore every Wednesday night was a big occasion both at Kirkby Stephen Low Station and Kirkby Stephen High Station.

Every week Anthony Allan bought 5 - 6 newly calved cattle to stand Hellifield on the Thursday, and it was generally my job to get his purchases home to Winton from North and South Stainmore, Kaber, Hartley, Brough, Brough Sowerby, Little Musgrave, etc. That was his main trading area. No cattle wagons, just Shanks Pony. Cattle in those days, all being home bred and tied up, were more docile than today's, and a great percentage had been taught to halter lead therefore, if so trained, you led them home. Maybe the dealer or farmer would be with you for the first half mile to see you were all right. If loose, that's when you learned your droving skills. First of all you had to determine who was the boss and then read their thoughts, which way they were going next, and beat them to it. Once settled down it was surprising how you managed and in those days with all the stock moved on the hoof, anyone who was near a road end, or gap or open gate stood and gave you a turn. Kaber Rigg was Open Common either side, no fences, just whin bushes. Once clear of Kaber Rigg, you felt better.

Every Wednesday night was the gathering up and dispatch night and

I was allowed out of school at 3pm half an hour early to help. First of all Bob Bentham, a drover man, used to walk from Kirkby Stephen to Winton where Anthony Allan had his cows ready, and Bob Bentham and I set off with them to Kirkby Stephen, where we picked up cows from the auction and sometimes other dealer's cattle. Then up to the Croglin Castle yard where we penned up next to the low station, LNER Darlington, Penrith, and Tebay line. We waited for the 4.30 train from Barnard Castle with the Hellifield dealer's cows from Tuesday, Middleton in Teesdale's auction and that day's Barnard Castle auction. Always there were two regular dealers, Stephen Thompson and Joe Hall. Joe always wore a hard hat, and another dealer sometimes with them was called Sam Brair. There would be maybe 2-3 wagons of new calved shorthorn cows, 8-10 per rail wagon to unload and set off with them and ours up to the High Station, LMS Carlisle-Leeds line, 3/4 mile distant to reload. The most I ever took part in was a drove of 67, and the Hellifield dealers always walked with us as they did all their travelling from Hellifield to Kirkby Stephen, Middleton, and Barnard Castle and back home by train. In winter time when it was dark early, often it was my job to be ahead with an oil storm lantern to warn any oncoming traffic.

When we arrived with our cattle at the top station we penned them, and the dealers and the station master, who all knew each other, always had a light hearted debate on how many wagons were needed. Were any cattle to go behind the slides, sheeted or non sheeted, and most of all, how little the fare? They had to pay before loading. One thing about the railway loading facilities, they were first class. The pens were all of strong wooden posts and thick bars, interconnecting gates between pens and the rail cattle wagon doors were so designed for easy loading. The wagons of cattle and the dealers went on the 6.30 passenger train to Hellifield where they were unloaded into the auction and made comfortable for the night, then made ready for the sale on the Thursday.

My pay was 1 shilling, 5p by today's rates, and the drover from Kirkby Stephen, BB, got 2 shillings, 10p by today's rates. Sometimes the other dealers gave you 3d or 6d depending how trade had been. One thing I always remember about Kirkby Stephen High Station, it was the coldest place I ever knew on a bad stormy night.

How much would Anthony Allan have invested? Say in one week he was sending 7 cows to Hellifield, not more than £120 for the lot. In those days it took a good light roan, well built, good udder, correct on all four quarters, easy to milk, 5-6 years old, newly calved, cocky horns, to make £26. That was the top price for the above type of cow and it would also have to have the red ticket for that days sale. Generally a lot of cows were in the £18-£23 mark and bidding went up by half crowns. But shorthorns, when you think, had nearly as many permutations as our new national lottery. Colour in order of value (my view): light roan, medium roan, dark grisly roan, blood red and white, blood red, light red and white, light red, ginger, and last of all white. If any had a black nose, it was considered very bad breeding. Horns had to be nice, quarter moon angle, cocky and light coloured, not too cocky as they would be termed Billy Goat horns. But there were horns of all angles. Young bulls wore horn trainers from say 6 months to full grown. You never knew what his true horns would have been like. Udders had to be of the right proportions. Four nice teats for milking, as all milking was still by hand. Other faults were teats like ice cream cornets, teats too small, knotted and chambered teats, light quarters due to hand milking, and udders from cat size to swill size. Four good legs and body in proportion and not too big in the head. If you had a white cow with a black nose you weren't in the top flight of farmers. Mastitis was very much a problem in the summer time especially among lying off cows. In those days it was called 'say ewer' (sore udder) and the main treatment was to strip out twice a day and rub bag and teats liberally with soft Stockholm tar or vaccadyne. The other four main diseases were calf picking (abortion), and Johnnes Disease and the Calf Youse (Husk), all which in later years were nearly eradicated. Abortion by improved hygiene and better government control of licensing of bulls, Johmes disease by TB testing and slaughter, and Calf Youse (Husk) by Dictol injections and (All's) ringworm by scrubbing brush plus liberal sump oil. General medicine was used as the only vet was at Kirkby Stephen, but he was nearly always too incapacitated to help! They were Alterine, Oxy Gas, Electra Fluid, and others. One product very much used by most dairy farmers was collodiom to seal newly calved cows teats to stop them leaking and this was used to x hours before presenting the animal for sale, making their udders larger and more milk producing potential looking.

Every farm had a medicine chest with some of the above. For foot rot it was a paste in a tin like shoe polish; Hilstons Foot Rot ointment from somewhere just over the Scotch border. There were also the other down points for your permutations: snuffed horn or horns, yuck doon, wooden leg, stifled, under or ower shot jaw, tight skinned, and goggly eyed. There were some good short horn herds in North Westmoreland, but we didn't excel around Winton.

In winter when the cattle had been brought inside, within 3 to 4 weeks they broke out with lice. The lice infecting them mostly on the head down their neck to their shoulders and sometimes along their back bone and the only remedy was (baccy dust) tobacco dust from the Druggist Browns, Kirkby Stephen. You bought it so much per pound, and using a home made shaker you dusted the parts of the animals infected, doing the job as quietly as possible, as only one small whiff up your nose set you off sneezing.

Anthony Allan was very keen on feeding his newly calved cows with buckets of warm bran mash and treacle and to warm them up before going to sale. He used to tell me to go with a bucket to the Bay Horse pub and get one gallon of beer barrel bottoms, the blacker and syrupier, the better; and the price was always one shilling. These he used to water down with warm water and give it to those who would drink it. Another stimulant was 6 drops of Aconite in water, but you had to drench it into the animal by a horn and this could make them shine.

The other most important product second to dairy cattle was the shorthorn bullock reared to sell at which age sulted your farm: six months old small stores, stirks 12-18 months, stronger stores, and 2-2 $1/_2$ years cattle suitable for finishing fat. The main diet for young calves was whole milk for 6 weeks then Sara consisting of blue milk with ground linseed and water for another 6 weeks; then for the next 6 weeks, just ground linseed with water, good hay being available from 1 month old. Crosfields and Calthorp were the first to make a calf gruel available and this was 90% ground linseed.

Now the big day of the year regarding bullocks was Luke Fair cattle sales, mid October. The first day was all clean female cattle suitable for breeding, wintering stores, feeding out or fat. The second day nothing but bullocks, but mostly strong bullocks needing anything from

6 months to 1 year feeding on, and this was the day the Lincolnshire, Suffolk, and Lancs dealers came and they made the trade. Names I can remember are Hancock, Girling, Ringer, and Barker. It was a sight to see them in droves of 60-100 going from the auction to the station. Each dealer's batch was as a matching bunch. Bullocks were reared with one purpose in mind; that whatever age you sold them to suit your farming programme, the proceeds were nearly always used to pay the rent. This was the number one priority for the farmer to know where his rent money was coming from. For having been able to pay the rent due was a big relief, and another year of farming to look forward to.

Now at the Low Station LNER, there was some activity; each dealer's drove had to be penned and loaded before the next drove arrived. These dealers had to book how many wagons they would require from Kirkby Stephen to their destination two days previous, so the railway authorities could get their cattle wagons to Kirkby Stephen ready and special trains arranged to remove them. The auctioneer at Kirkby Stephen Mart was Edwin Huck and one trainee auctioneer Joe Cleasby. The mart foreman was Jack Swift who was a bit of a character. He had an impediment in his speech; and if he couldn't make you understand what he was shouting, he made sure by how he handled his stick. Another regular mart man was Harry Barker; Harry was there every Monday morning with his bucket, curry comb and brush. Can I clean your cow up mister? I think he charged 1 shilling and he was quite a good hand at making up a cow. T Bousfield of Hartley Fold milked all the cows after being sold and his word was respected on any disputes.

Kirkby Stephen had a good catchment area, all stock coming in on the hoof from Mallerstang, Fell End, Ravonstonedale, Crosby Garrett, Asby, Soulby, Musgrave, Brough, Warcop, Stainmore, Kaber, Winton, and Hartley. On the main special sale days cattle and sheep from the most outlying areas were brought to around Kirkby Stephen, Winton, and Hartley the day previous, so they only had a short drive on the sale day.

For everything you sold you were expected to give luck money to the purchaser, and the dealers knew who was generous, careful, or refused and they would bid accordingly. As the years went by, the luck to be given on newly calved cows got out of hand. Now two ways of dealing which were very much to the fore in those days were: (how much to join) say the farmer had a cow which he thought was worth £20, he may get another farmer or dealer to join at £20, and if it made £22 he owed the person joining £1, and if it made £18, the person joining owed him £1. It was not very often that the person joining had to pay, but for the seller it gave him a guarantee of somewhere near where he wanted to be. Auctions in the 30's were a lot more erratic than they are today. Some days if trade was bad, 50% could pass through unsold. The other way for more selling at home or at the horse fair was (to boot), 'barter'- you had an animal or animals to sell but you wanted to trade them in against what you were requiring, rather like the car trade of today, so after inspecting each others animals, the one with the greater value started off with how many £s (to boot) 'barter' would you give. Never heard of today was what they called 'Paddy's Drop'. This was someone asking an exorbitant price and you bid him half of his asking price, but here again you could be caught out. Another type of Dealing - 'for life', if the vendor gave it out to the auctioneer that the animal or animals he was selling for life meant that whoever bought them had no redress whatsoever on the vendor. Whatever fault or faults he found out. Generally it could be a horse that was a 'dead wrong 'un' or a cow or heifer unmilkable. Or animals that were unsteerable, dyke broken. The dealers would bid accordingly when 'for life' was given out, but the vendor had the peace of mind that they couldn't come back at him.

Throw Them Up

In the 30s, selling a new calved cow by auction was quite a harrowing experience as among the new calved cow dealers there were some who had not a very reputable manner. If they thought the farmer selling was, in their terms, easy meat, they would buy his cow and then ask for excessive luck money and then on some feeble pretext, be it supposed to be light of a quarter or hard to draw, etc, they would demand £x else they would throw the cow up. The auction company tolerated them as they could be the main buyers at that weekly auction. But R R Sowerby of Winton House, Winton, took the wind out of the dealers' sails. When showing a cow at Penrith for his first time and these dealers bought it and whether they thought RR was an easy touch dressed in plus fours and brogues, they started on him that his cow had this and that faults. R R listened to them and then said, 'Are you finished?' By then quite a crowd had gathered around. 'Well gentlemen, you have had your say, now I'll have mine. First of all, as well as being a farmer, I am a solicitor and as far as you and my cow which you now own, I brought it into a public auction for sale and it was on display for all to see. I did not tell you to bid for it, therefore so as far as I am concerned, that if you didn't notice all these faults you say it has, it must have been very poor judgment on your part. So as far as I am concerned, I have nothing more to say'. He, that day, did a good job for the ordinary farmer.

Going to the other extreme, this day Joseph Richardson asked would I give him a hand to take a newly calved cow to Kirkby Stephen auction and it went through the ring and in those days whoever was showing the cow followed it out of the ring and back to its stall. After we had tied it up, the dealer, Stephen Thompson came down and said, 'Now Joseph, is your cow right and straight?' and Joseph replied, 'She is'. 'Well, just give me a shilling to make her lucky. You know you and I have known each other too long to start telling lies.'

Now the greatest season of the year and very important to the farmer and the cattle was hay time. Whether the hay was got good or badly, that was the animals food for the next winter. Also if it was a bad summer, you didn't get your meadows cleared, there was no second flush of grass, fog, for the autumn.

Hay time was governed to how many acres you could handle, was what you had for horses and manual labour. First extra labour; you could hire an extra Irishman for 4 weeks. They used to come into Heysham mid/late June and walk or hitch a ride to the Dales for the local market days. Kirkby Stephen was always on a Monday. They would hire for a month and have to lead the way and always got the hardest job. But no Sunday working; Sunday morning you could see them making for Appleby the nearest RC Church. Some came year after year to the same farm; and the wage for a month for a good reliable man was £8. The local lads used to complain as their wages were only £26 for the half year, i.e. just over £4 per month. But the Irish lads were always put in at the hard end, the main gamble with hiring for a month was the weather. If it was bad and catchy, you didn't get your full value and maybe some hay still to get when their month was up. The other local pool of labour was the night man. The three main local industries were Hartley Quarries, the Railway, and the council road men; and I would say over 80% of these men had farming experience. Finishing roughly their own job at approx. 5pm so on a good night 6pm-11pm they were good value at 1s per hour, as that time of day was nearly always the busiest. Also the farmers wives and servant girls although busy making extra meals etc. turned out for any hand rake work suitable for them. Regarding horsepower the larger farms were all right; they could produce 2 good horses for the double horse mowing machine; the number one method of cutting grass. Those with only 1 horse could either hire a horse for hay time, £3 per month to make a pair, or join up with their neighbour who only had 1 horse to make a team for a 2 horse machine and cutting grass for each alternately. There were single horse machines but you required a stronger, bigger type of horse to our fell ponies as they were a hard draught. Horses could be hired at £3 per month from Dan Sowerby or Watty Allison.

The size of each mowing was governed by the size of your labour force; if small fields of up to 2 acres, 1 cutting. Anything bigger divided into platts; the size of platts handed down from father to son. To cut a field different than the old platt size was a local talking point. Weight of hay crop varied but even a good crop was a long way short of today's single cut but it stood up better as it was a greater mix of grasses and herbs. But it had its problem if taken too sharp and green and the biggest danger was heating up and taking fire. Sink Mows with 4 enclosed walls were the most dangerous, so all sink mows either had a wooden rail chimney in the centre or they had a rope with a sack of hay on the end tied to a beam and this sack was pulled up the centre as the Mow was filled making a chimney. Short herby mixtures were the most dangerous. If it had been gaily warm it came out brown, but if it had been next door to firing it came out black with a lovely smell, nearly like new cut plug tobacco. The cattle and sheep loved it brown and black and up to 6 weeks were reckoned the most dangerous period. The only fert it had, if any, was the manure from eating last years crop, even so where even this poor manure had been applied you could tell it to an inch. The old saying; 'Nothing is more honest than land.' Mowing if the weather was settled was always done very early morning when coolest say from 6 am to 9/10 ish. Some had the reputation of mowing through the night. One farmer just out of Kirkby Stephen was joked about that they came in at 11 pm one night, washed, had their supper and went to bed; and the hired lad had an extra big knot in his clog laces, and by the time he got it untangled and set of up the stairs the farmer was coming down to start again. If the weather was good, making it into hay was straightforward, but in catchy weather, first turned then strewn out and then into small cocks, then break them out into large cocks or jockeys cocks, break out again, next into pikes, haystack, or home building, or field house. Moving the hay was the major job; if to a stack or field house or pikes sweeping with a one horse or two horse gate sweep or tipping Tom, if to the homestead by block cart with shelvings properly loaded, roped, and raked down before leaving the hay field. Most farmers took a pride in how their loads of hay looked going into the village. If your farm was big enough and you could have 3 horses and carts; one loading in the field, one unloading at home, and one on the road in between home and field, you were moving some hay. Remember all the hay was loose, no balers at all. The other hay time machines were a side delivery rake which could be made to turn as well. If your farm was big enough a strawer and horse rake. The main hand tools were hay forks and hay rakes, ginny rake, and scythes. One main snag with horse implements was that they were wider than the gateways; every time you moved through any gates, unyoke, handhandle the machine sideways through the gate, and yoke up again. So whenever a gate wanted renewing, a wider gate with stoops set wider was a must. If the landlord could be persuaded to buy the new gate.

As the grasses years ago were of a different composition from todays, which are now mostly Rye grass and Timothy, yesterdays were of a herby and clover mixture in the meadow and pastures were a far larger variety of different grasses.

Towards 1938 old cars were little money say £5, and you were getting modern if you bought one. One farmer had an Armstrong Siddeley with dickie seats and the same time Gelders of Longmarton started a revolution in hay sweeps to fit to these cars with ten long pitch pine prongs. Later tractors very straightforward to attach, not very popular with the Irishmen, no breathers for them when the horse had a breather. Another farmer, L Metcalfe, Hewgill House, Winton bought a Morris

Oxford, a large saloon car, cut the body off, just leaving the front seat intact, fitting a horse cart body on the rear portion plus shelvings; the first motorised general purpose vehicle to cart the hay, cart manure, and sweep in the district.

If it came dodgy weather the first job was to make all ready again for off; machine knives sharpened, all machines well oiled, horses rested etc; but the main job which nobody seemed to rush to was forking back the hay moos, hay which had settled down in the buildings or Dutch barns or lofts was all mooed into timber lengths. Every main cross beam across the building determined a timber length. Good dry hay could settle between a third or quarter of its height overnight therefore as your moos settled you had to keep forking them back to make full use of the space by filling them up to the roof baulks again. If at a field house and it was a good crop year and it wouldn't hold the hay that day, you made a pike of the surplus hay under the forking hole and came back after it had settled and fork it in. One other job when hay time was finished was pulling the hay moos; all the fronts of the moos had to be pulled/plucked dead straight; as the boss would say, 'make them look as someone owned them.' When I first went along to the farm Anthony Allen had a long large blue Morris Cowley with running boards, and the windows were celluloid which slotted onto the top of the doors, and a large brass dome shaped radiator. Then Anthony changed it for the same model but red. But in 1936 Ford brought out their Ford 8 'Popular' family car, brand new, taxed and insured on the road £100. So he bought one, ran it for a year, then traded it in for £90 and for another £10 just the same model, price £100. He ran it for a year but in 1938 Ford brought out the Prefect, £120, so he traded again to get the new Prefect. Sadly 1939 brought the new car trade to an halt so how long he ran the Prefect I couldn't say.

Now how were the cattle housed? Well first of all bedding straw was a luxury, the only bedding used was for calves until they were say 3 - 4 months old. Some farmers did grow oats but the straw was nearly always used for fodder. Bracken or sieves if available locally or bad inedible hay was the main types of bedding. The bracken and sieve cutting was an early autumn job. Now, as all animals from 3 - 4 months were tied up either rope or chain cow bands were used and different sized stalls were needed so you maybe had a small stirk byre, a young beasts byre, and cow byres. The byres were nearly always part of a barn. The byre supporting the floor above with sink moo adjoining the byre. The byres were all paved out with paving stones, but in the 1930's the better farmer was improving his byres by uplifting the paving stones behind the cows in the grope and walkway and cementing level; making it a lot easier for shoveling the dung out. Also farmers who wanted more byre room at home built byres along the side of the barn making use of the barn wall for one wall and sometimes knocking out the byre loft part of the barn to make more room for his hay crop.

Well how did you water your stock? Well on one or two of the larger farms water bowls were being fitted but only for the milk cows at first as it was solid piping, a lot of work, and expensive; no plastic piping as now. Your other main supply was the village beck, and if you had to follow Winton beck from say where it crosses the first fell lane, down to Beck-A-Waden where it joined the river Eden and see how our forefathers had utilized the beck. Some thought had gone into it, the number of fields that had been given access to must have been master planned, and the walls and hedges made to fit the beck. In North Westmoreland the beck or river was the first consideration, a water or good spring supply for village or farm.

When you come into the village itself, village not parish; out of the 22 farms and small holdings, 14 has direct access on their own land from their buildings to the beck for watering purposes. The other holdings had access to the beck out of the village down by the public house down to the beck where it was open plan up to the Mill gate; and it was a sight to remember seeing the teens of cattle drinking overlapping each up the beck up to the Mill gate to keep getting clear water. And when clear of cattle it ran clear again in one or two minutes ready for the next lot of cattle. Some farms had a piped water or pumped trough in the farm yard but letting two cattle out at a time was a slow job. Where you had a field house cattle had often to walk some considerable distance to the nearest beck, spring, or pond. And where it was a pond you had to go and check it in hard weather to make sure it wasn't iced up. Other cattle than milk cows were only let out once per day for watering.

Tying at the back end was nearly always left until a very bad day weather wise and the stock were pleased to come in for the shelter and they soon all learned the watering procedures and their own stalls. You had to get a move on while they were out at water, settle stones to brush down, boos heads also to brush out, and each animal its correct amount of hay.

Now in spring time that was all different, they only had to taste one blade of green grass and they forgot all about coming back in and you either had to be a good runner, or you had a good cattle dog.

Land without access to natural water was farmed to need the least amount of water carting to it. If possible it was ploughed or meadowed, and if used for livestock as stated water was carted to it as a backup measure. But most of the time the farmer only let them graze that field for four to six hours per day, bringing them back to where he had natural water available for them.

It was a big deterrent to land without natural water when up for sale or renting. Now as regards the village horses you would have bet that the most of them would have been fell ponies or dales ponies, but to find a true fell/dales pony you had to go on to Stainmore or Mallerstang, or any farms up out of the villages.

You had two types of farmers, one which when they bought a young horse and it suited him he would keep it his lifetime and it would become part of the family, and if it was a mare and he had enough grazing he would breed from it to sell surplus, a yearling or as a two year old. The other type of farmer made his horses do the farm work, mares he would breed off, and for other horses he had either his own stags or bought young 3 to 4 year old stags to break in; selling them when fully broken for chain or cart work. He was maybe more of a horseman than farmer. He always had to be breaking and training young horses. And there was money to be made, the difference between a broken and unbroken horse could be £10-£12, a good investment considering you got you work done as well. To produce a good black well broken Vanner, 4-5 years old, ready to go into the towns for van work, always made a premium and one thing these horsemen used to tell us lads; never break a young horse unless it was in a good fit fighting condition, any faults or badness were more likely to come out then.

My memories of the Winton horses were Tommy Allen, Anthony Allen's faithful horse was a pure Galloway, how it came down from the Scottish Galloway Hills was maybe by some of the Dumfries or Castle Douglas boys on their way to Appleby or Brough Fair had brought him down to be sold. Tommy was a very intelligent horse, Anthony Allen's Uncle Jim was over 80 years old and Jim used to get onto a low wall which had railings on the top and Tommy used to lean over sideways to make it easier for uncle Jim to mount, he did the same when he wanted to dismount.

Now when I rode him bareback with only a halter and in the right type of field to get him galloping, but Tommy only stood so much. Maybe you had only gone 50 yards when he would put on his four anchors and head down leaving you only one place to go, and then he just started grazing as if nothing had happened. Tommy was Anthony Allen's main workhorse and was always in demand to do other jobs. Any villagers who wanted something carted, whether it was furniture, firewood, farm manure, etc. used to borrow Tommy and his cart. Another job for which he was required was to be the anchor horse when yoking a young horse double for the first time, especially in the double mowing machine. One job I always remember, was Eddie Hird. A local man who had got married and had taken the job as general farm man with Phillip Rudd, Broom Rigg Farm, Langrigg. The cottage with the job was on the A66, just at the bottom of Gatehouse Brow. So one fine summer evening with Tommy and cart, we loaded up his household goods, ex the cottage attached to Barker House where he had lived with his mother and sister, and it was my job after delivering and unloading the household goods, to drive Tommy back to Winton so that Eddy could stay at his new abode. As Anthony Allen always had two fell type breeding mares heathed on Winton Fell, come February and when the weather was hard, maybe once a week, they received a fothering of hay and on a Friday night AA would say, Line your mate up for the morning. You can go and fother the fell ponies. As my schoolmate was Geordie Taylor we were down at AA's next morning and with Tommy and two bags of hay strung over his withers and Geordie and me on board always bareback, off we went to fother the fell ponies and AA's last instructions were, 'Remember to find a lowen spot to fother them in'.

Wharton Steel's horse was called Captain and his novelty was to bite off your cap gently and hold it in his mouth.

Now Cowards of Manor House Farm had 3 or 4 large Clydesdales for their ploughing etc, but everyone's good friend was Daisy, not so much a big pony, but as Joe and Martin were getting on in years it was her job with the small flat cart to be their getaround and she had her own stable and stall away from the main stable in with the young calves. Daisy with the Get Around Cart for Martin and Joe had at least in summer time two longish weekly trips. For as farmed along with Manor House were two large allotments: one the Kirkby Stephen golf links with access from the lane from the bottom of Wiseber and the other Hayter Gill with access from the road between Red Gate Farm, Rookby and Heggarscale.

Marstons, South View, now everyone knew Pansy, not a very big Clydesdale but a lovely roaned colour.

P H Dent, Hilltop, his horse was called Fanny, a nice black cob, and its field day every month or so was to bring a load of coals approx 7 cwt from the low station, Kirkby Stephen for the school, and the rate for the job was 2/6d.

The four local blacksmiths were; A Wilson, Mellbecks; J Whitehead, Nateby Road, Kirkby Stephen; G Adamtwaite, Gt Musgrave; and T. Sayer, Brough Sowerby. I can just remember Winton Smithy being demolished.

The three main horse dealers I can remember were; Watson('Watty') Allison, The Mill, Church Brough; Mut Atkinson, Crackenthorpe, Appleby; and W J Dent, Kaber Fold; but there were others as well. Horse dealing was quite a big business, nearly every month there would be cart horse sales at Penrith, Carlisle, and Wigton auctions for the cream of the horse trade. But our three local fairs for any type of horse were Appleby Fair, early June; Cowper Day Fair, Kirkby Stephen in the streets, the end of September; and Brough Hill Fair on the A66 between Brough and Warcop the day after Cowper Day.

Apparently Brough Hill Fair also had a day for cattle as well, but I only knew it when there was only horses, and it was always laid down that shod horses were down on the road the A66, and other types of horses were on the hill. One recollection I have on the horse side was a horse dealer called Bert Richardson from Bishop Auckland who had to start with in the morning with up to 50 untouched 2/3 year old Clydesdale stags. He would shout out 'pick out the one you fancy, they are all for sale,' There would be men there to halter them and show you their paces. He had come for years and had a good name and regular customers looking for horses to break in. W Allison of Church Brough was the main dealer bringing lots of Irish horses into our area, just that bit larger and stronger than our fell/dales ponies. He would go over to the Irish fairs and buy 35-40 horses, nearly all broken, and ship them from Ireland to Heysham, and then 2 day walking from Heysham to Church Brough. On the 2 day trek from Heysham to Church Brough they stopped for one night at Hollybush farm, Casterton, Kirkby Lonsdale where Henry Bownass farmed as a farmer/dealer. On their arrival at the farm mid afternoon Henry selected 5 or 6 horses out for orders he had around his area and then with the help of his nephew, Edmund and others the selected horses were first yoked and tried doing chain work, then yoked into block carts and finally tried whilst still yoked in the block cart with the wheels locked to make sure they weren't jibbers. And if they acted reasonably well even if they were a bit green or skittish he purchased them. The rest of the horses were well looked after for the night ready for the 2nd days trek to Church Brough and another stageing post for horses going over the top was Gilling West near Scotch Corner. He always made sure he had plenty for hay time to sell or rent out as this was the time of year farmers always made sure their horse power was adequate for hay time. In other words he was a 'used horse salesman!' taking your horse if you wanted in part exchange; apparently in the first world war he had been a big buyer of horses for the British army. Daniel Sowerby, Sun Inn, Kirkby Stephen always did some horse trade pre hay time, but his was mostly horses for hire, £3 per month. W J Dent, Kaber Fold was also a keen horse breaker and dealer, plus Anthony Allen and these two always had some stags or other horses for the 3 local fairs. If they thought they hadn't enough they would buy some the day before. It was part of their life, they must have horses to take to the fairs, and Brough Hill Fair was the number 1 for Anthony Allan. Three or four to the fair and nearly always one for me to bring back. He always found one with a shilling still in it.

In approximately 1936 Morecambe Corporation closed down their horse drawn trams. The horses were sold by auction. They were offered in working pairs. Duke and Duchess, Actor and Actress, Prince and Princess, Count and Countess, etc. and the worst trait they had with their new owners was they knew nothing but walking right up the middle of the road. A purchaser from Ingleton left his son to walk two home and some fun he had!

The other main farm income was sheep and as regards breeds, not much different from today. Pure Swaledale, pure Wensleydale, for crossing the Swaledale for half bred lambs. The Tees Water was just in its infancy. Some farmers were beginning to look at them. As Winton and Kaber Fell were stinted for sheep and horses, every farm or holding in Winton and Kaber Parishes had X Stints rights on the above fell, according to how many acres of in bye land they had in the Parishes. But as these stints were saleable the very smallholdings to just to have a very small number of stock on the fell and so far away and you just couldn't put them through the fell gate, they were heathed stock being reared on that section of fell and which shepherded confined to that section. Therefore unless you had a flock of 40 or more it was uneconomical to farm them, but whenever these stints came up for sale, the person of the adjoining heath was always ready to buy them and at the sale the other stint holders made sure he didn't beg them. There was something about fell rights. There were many arguments in the village in the 30s. There were only perhaps 10 active holders, now I believe only 2. A bigger proportion of the Swales were kept pure. Only the better lower farms went in for half bred lamb production and the Wensleydale were only kept on 2 farms in the village just a flock of 4 or 5 for tup lamb production. On sheep sales, very much as today, starting early September on the half bred lambs, only difference in those days both Gimmer and Wethers were sold the same day to make it a big day. Prices for a very top pen of Gimmers, £2-2/6d each. General rule top Gimmers £2. Following sales crossed, black faced ewes, store wether lambs, then uncrossed ewes, tup sales. Ewes anywhere from 5s to £2. A very good tup shearling, £5. Novelty ones up to £50. And finally Luke Fair. All Kirkby Stephen penned from Hartley Road end to Brougham Lane and it was termed the sweeping up day for any type any age of sheep, it was a big day for the sheep men. Some store and fat lambs, these you could sell on the market day sales. The only difference to now is that the Udales and Ellwoods and others bought local and took the fat lambs to the town's auction to sell to the town butchers and also bought a lot of store lambs to fatten on their own farms. Or took fields of turnips to fatten them. Appleby/Penrith area was a big area for turnips. Trainloads of half bred in lamb ewes from the Skipton area came from December to early March at so much per sheep per week and local stations Appleby Kirkby Thore, Temple Sowerby, Cliburn, Clifton and Penrith were used. Prices of good store black faced lambs, 16s - 17s each. When fat, 23 - 24s each. Good store half breed lamb, 22 - 23s each, 30 - 32s each, fat. But in those days they had to be big and could not be too fat. Drenches as today were unheard of and there seemed to be a bigger proportion of shots, small lambs, unsaleable but nicely overwintered and if they survived Doctor Green. They summered to sell as breeders or fat shearlings. Maybe 2 or 3 half bred Gimmers, nicely marked helped to make the top pen of lambs at main sale.

Re Village Life

I would say out of the 52 going to school there were nearly 20 lads who lived in the village and when we weren't doing our jobs after school hours nearly everyone had jobs at home or elsewhere to do before being allowed back out to play. We had to make our own pleasure and pastime. Different times of year, we just changed from one thing to another. But, when first at school you had to have a booley and the miles you boolied, was quite some mileage. Whips and tops was quite a game to master. Who could lift a top the furthest and the main street was our playground. The two main types of tops were the mushroom and beehive. Marbles had their turn. Glass alleys being the most sought after, played up the gutter and keeping a sharp look out for drains. Conker time was fixed by nature and the methods for curing and making hard, nearly everyone had a different recipe. As regards how many timer your conker was, was very open to debate. Footballing was governed by the availability of a football. Clogs didn't give them a long life and the green was our pitch. Two trees were the goal posts at the top end and at the bottom one tree and someone's' jacket. We had a good pal in J Coward from Manor House Farm. He was the local village handyman, semi veterinary. He used to keep us supplied with pig bladders when killing pigs for the locals in winter time. Cricket used to get a turn in summer, but our pitch, the green, with too many windows near, restricted it. There was a strict rule, windows broken, had to be paid for. Sledging in winter down the road from the Pun Fold to at least the Chapel if conditions were right. At times we used Winton Hall Pastures on the road to Whingill but were restricted where we could sledge, plenty of hills but too many stone walls at the bottom. We had a good grapevine. Somebody always knew when G Hullock with his steam engine and thresher was coming. It was an education to watch George handling his massive steam engine in tight stack yards and if things weren't going just right his language isn't in the English dictionary. Also we knew when the County Council steam engine and stone breaking outfit was passing on it way from Helbeck Quarry to either Tail Bridge or Fell End quarries. If there was in summer time any special activities such as yoking a young horse for the first time, or haltering stags, these were generally after night milking when there was help available. We were there.

Other seasonal activities were such as walking the beck in March/April, maybe there were 6 or 7 different people who kept ducks. These were housed every night and they were kept in the next morning until they had laid their eggs, before being let out to go back to the beck, there were always two or three who preferred to lay when on the beck and were claimed by who first spotted them. The most prominent breed were Kaki Campbells and others were white Aylesbury and Moscovies. These ducks every day all made their way down to the River Eden and when coming home at darking, each lot knew just where to leave the beck for their own homestead.

Also, re the beck, in Spring on the higher Parish reaches, there was a good crop of water cress. Mushrooming was another seasonal activity, first in the pastures and then the fog ones, and on these as lads we were only left the tailings with quite a lot of men in the village and Kirkby Stephen on shift work, they were out by the crack of dawn. They knew the best fields and with a usual average crop they could make 4d a pound, to the local produce merchants to send over to Darlington or Newcastle, picked really early then on to the 11.30 a.m.

Darlington train and in the shops that afternoon. In a very good crop year with too many about, prices could collapse to 2d or even 1d a lb.

Another activity we used to enjoy was potato picking (scratting tatties). Three farms in the village were into ploughing: Manor House, Windy Gate and South View, and Manor House had maybe 2 or 3 acres of potatoes so up to 10 or 12 of us got a job there mid October tattie week, weather permitting. But you had to be at least 8 years old and the pay was 1/- per day, but you got your coffee, dinner and tea in the field as there was no potato diggers, the horse man with his two Clydesdales with a stitching plough used to split a stitch open into 2 halves and it was your job to scrat the potatoes out and place in a swill and another horseman with his cart emptied your swills and the two owners of the farm brothers Martin Coward and Joseph Coward, both had small metal rakes with nail like teeth and they followed up the stitch, making sure none was missed. If they found any, they shouted and the nearest of you had to go and pick them up. They were very traditional farmers. Everything prim and proper and when it was time to knock off, say 4 o'clock, Martin used to stand in the gateway of the potato field and gave us all our pay for the day - 1/-. He often used to remark when paying, don't forget lads, always remember in life to pay and be paid.

Poultry

Well, the two main ways of producing poultry were either by setting clockers on their eggs or by incubators, the Glevum paraffin 100 egg size being the main one and all farms, small holdings and house holders kept hens. Poultry was when well cared for, a contribution to all household expenses.

Depending upon how poultry minded you were, they were kept in flocks from say 10 to 200, but if you were in the 150-200 flock size, you were quite big among the poultry keepers. Layers were kept in lots of 30 to 40 per hen house, the hen houses room placed round the garth and home pasture and house holders without land, on the village common, or by arrangement with neighbouring farmers on their pastures. On feeding they had to have a hot crowdy early morning, mainly consisting of either sharps, thirds, pollards, wheatfeed or Indian Meal, plus fish meal, pea meal or bean meal for protein, plus the famous Karswood Poultry spice and an evening feed of say oats, wheat, whole maize or cut maize.

Eggs were sold by the score (20) for eating and by 15 when for hatching. In the spring when they used to say any old sort of hen laid and eggs were at their cheapest increasing in price through the summer to being their dearest in winter, and nearly every household bought eggs in the spring when cheapest to preserve in water glass to use in the winter months.

Now on breeds of hens; there were many but the most profitable for eggs were the leghorns, the white, the brown, and the black; but a bit flighty and a small carcass. For table or dual purpose the Rhode Island Red, the Light Sussex, White Wynedotte, Barred Rock, and others. The main problem when hatching was what percentage of your chickens were cock chickens, and by the time the chicks were 6 to 7 weeks old you could pick the cocks out by their combs and the good poultry keeper separated them from the pullets and kept them separate to fatten off. Actually cock chicken pie was often on the menu from say June onwards depending on the breed you farmed, and the good poultry man had a number of point of lay pullets to replace x number of old hens every back end, of which the old hens were either boiled or roasted for your own consumption or sold weekly to the produce merchant.

Two aspects of poultry keeping which nobody was so keen on, but if you were the hired hand you were sure to get them, were: first, cleaning the hen houses out every week or ten days. Perches and dropping board first cleaned, nest, boxes re hayed, and then the main floor cleaned and dusted with lime dust, then having to empty your barrow, and finally scaling the manure. The other aspect was dealing with clockers, broodies if they were not required for hatching, they had to be banished and the two main ways were either to put them into a sheep rack, where they could not sit or put into a hessian sack and hung up a tree. Both cleaning out and banishing clockers had always been an afternoon job so that early in the day you didn't disturb their laying pattern, and you could guarantee that you felt cooty even if you weren't 'cooty' after cleaning out the hen houses.

Now to clear the surplus eggs, old hens, cock chickens, old cockerels, rabbits and butter etc., we in the Winton/Kirkby Stephen area had four good produce merchants: Tom Wilson, Silver Street, Kirkby Stephen; Tim Pighills, Soulby; Kit Currah of Warcop; and Dalston Alderson, Brough. They all had different days weekly going round their customers buying produce, eggs, butter, hens, rabbits, etc. to send by that day's evening train to the North East, Darlington, Newcastle. They altered their prices up or down according to supply and demand, so they were always greeted by 'Now how much are you paying today?' and it was the tradesman's custom to pay cash and their coins were always carried in a leather bag with a drawstring at the top to close it. Notes were placed in an expandable wallet with elastic straps. Put the note in the open centre of the wallet, turn it over one way then the other way and the note was safely in behind the elastic straps and this weekly produce merchants cash was the house keeping money for the week. The other main line they purchased was rabbits. Always by the couple and they would check each couple to make sure they were good clean and average size. Depending on the time of year say from August to March stating off in August one shilling a couple, by December up to 2 shillings a couple and after Christmas when rabbits were getting scarce, up to 2/6 per couple. The poor rabbit was classed as a pest but in reality it was the country dwellers best friend. Maybe on some of the sandy farms there were too many and they ate some crops but in general every Spring you thought there were no rabbits left but come early summer they appeared, spread out over their old haunts, but many a family had many meals of roast rabbit and rabbit pie. At no cost, you just had to catch one and nothing tasted better. Most hired lads and hired married men knew how to catch them, either by ferreting, snaring or with a good nose dog on the higher ground following the walls. Shooting and gin trapping were not all that popular. Catching a rabbit or two every week was a good supplement to your pocket money, or it was your pocket money, your own hop and skip bank but you had to have the knack and knowledge to draw your money out. On some farms, not many, where the rabbits were in great numbers the farmer would let off his farm to a professional rabbit catcher, either x pence per couple caught, or a fixed sum for the right to catch all the rabbits on his farm for the season. It was said some farmers paid the rent out of the rabbits.

The produce men always lowered their prices for shot, trapped and flood rabbits. Flood rabbits were when the Eden was in flood and their burrows water logged. The boys with their lurchers, whippets and terriers soon cleaned up the rabbits on a big flood. The produce men and other tradesmen due to the LNER from Darlington to Kirkby Stephen did a lot of trade both ways with the North East. More so than down the valley with Penrith and Carlisle. Going over Stainmore to the North East was 'Garn o'er top'. Now as regard all the other tradesmen who came round, I can remember most of them.

Butchers:

W. Marston, Kirkby Stephen. The only one I can remember who always had a blood-type horse and proper butchers gig.

J D Hall, Kirkby Stephen. A Model T Ford van.

A Chapman, Kirkby Stephen

J Longstaff, Soulby

J Milburn, Church Brough

D Atkinson, Brough

Porky Dowson, Appleby - nothing but pork, bacon, ham and potted meat

Coalmen

All stations sold coal. For Winton, Kirkby Stephen or Great Musgrave, people namely farmers wouldn't go to the station unless they knew there was a wagon of Glasshoughton best in, and the first bagged delivered coal I remember was from Evenwood, Bishop Auckland, every fortnight, 1s per bag, and E Bousfield and J. Cooper started selling coals in Kirkby Stephen by motorised transport.

Ice-cream

Percy Bellezza from Shildon, with his motor bike and side car just summer months, 1/2d and 1d cornets and 1d sandwiches. Everyone knew Percy's whistle every Tuesday night.

Grocers

From Kirkby Stephen, Hastwells, the Co-op, Walter Wilson, and from Brough Hilton Stores, their travellers on their bicycles one day, the provisions delivered on the following day. Walter Wilsons and Hilton Stores were the last to use horses and they had special flat carts for carrying mostly boxes of provisions. W. Anderson had the main village shop, everything weighed and packed as you bought it, open from 8 a.m. until 10 p.m. He stocked everything within reason for a village shop. Billy Anderson had one thing in common with Henry Ford - that was that Henry used to say, you can have your vehicle any colour you like as long as it was black. Now Billy didn't say it, but whatever thickness you asked to have your bacon, Billy had only one thickness (thick). His flick of bacon hung above his till and when Billy took it down onto the counter he would say how many slices do you require and with his large black handled gully, he would cut the number of slices required. And on twist tobacco from the coil, the length from his thumb end to his elbow was 1 ounce, black or brown 3p per ounce. Paraffin was a major commodity. There was another shop just for pop and sweets run by Mrs. Johnny Sowerby, the middle house of Fell View Terrace. There were some houses on RR Sowerby's electric supply from the Mill Wheel down at the Mill but most cottage houses didn't have electricity until 1936 when Johnson and Philip brought the grid to Winton. It was 1s in the slot. You paid before you received any. Everyone had to have 1s in reserve as when your 1s was done out went the lights. When the meter men came round to empty the meters they gave back to the owner, sometimes 1s out of every 10s, and the householders didn't mind him coming. Now the shop also sold paraffin but you had to go and collect and take your own drum but Bob Nixon who was a part time postman who lived on King's Terrace gave a delivery service, not only to Winton Parish, but also neighbouring parishes. His AJS motor cycle with its box side car was a regular sight and then Bob went up market. He purchased a second hand Austin 7 saloon car and converted it into a small truck. Its top load wouldn't be more than 30 gallons but Bob was more sheltered from the inclement weather. Another weekly service was Mr. Hall from the bungalows down Appleby road from Kirkby Stephen with his wet batteries. Before electric came not many people had a wireless and they had to be connected up to a dry battery and a wet battery which needed to be recharged every week. The size of the wet battery was say 3 and a half inches square, and 6 inches high. Mr. Hall had adapted his carrier on his bicycle a frame to hold 6 batteries and as he had a small water wheel at his bungalow where he recharged them going on his rounds he gave a weekly replacement and I think his charge was 6d in old money. The dry battery was quite expensive, 4s, which was a lot of money, so if the wireless was off the dry battery was flat and it was a case of where the 4s was coming from to replace it. Another regular was Benny Fisher from Brough with his bicycle and small box sidecar and he sold 1/4 lb packets of tea and 1/2 lbs of margarine. Dan Sowerby Sun Inn Kirkby Stephen used to come round with his horse and flat cart with boxes of fresh herring when in season. 1s per pound 'Fresh Herring, Fresh Herring, Fine Big Fresh Herring' was his cry and you knew you had to provide your own plate, the job didn't run to greaseproof paper. My younger brother, Ivan, was Dan's right-hand man and as we lived at the bottom of the village where Dan used to start from, all Saturdays or holiday time he would pick up my brother, stand him on his cart to shout his wares. Dan was also the main scrap dealer from Kirkby Stephen. He and others used to have their rounds collecting scrap metal, horse hair, sheep daggings, rabbit skins, mole skins, and used sacks. They had a price for anything and Dan used to have his scrap yard down Hartley Road and when it was full and the price right Vickers of Barrow used to come with their lovely green painted and brass fitted wagons. A sight to see. He was also a horse trader and hired horses out for different jobs, mainly for hay time. The others like Dan were Jack Sowerby, North Road, his field come yard was where the new Co-op Superstore is. There was also Tom Varey, Hartley Road, and Jack Walsh, Saur Pow. You could always tell where they owned any land; they used for fencing lovely metal bed ends with all their brass fittings. Just what every antique dealer is now looking for. And in summertime when out on their rounds they always had on their flat cart a scythe and before returning they nearly always found some grass on the roadside to cut. Maybe not a lot but enough to keep his horse until another day. Main lines collected when out hawking, horse hair very profitable and used sacks. This sack trade getting larger year by year with more feeding stuffs being purchased.

Late back end would see the onion men with their sit up and beg bikes loaded down with straps of onions, calling at every house, approximately 20 onions per strap. A strap was always hung in the kitchen, cutting them off one by one as required.

They were all very much alike: tall, thin and wiry, dressed in dark trousers and a long type black jacket and black beret type cap. How they travelled up as far North as North Westmoreland I never knew. There was no chance of them riding their bikes. Without a saddle, the bike was just a mode of transport for the onions, and to have come over the Channel from Brittany, they were certainly out with their bikes to make a living.

Bicycles

Bicycles were the main means of transport, of getting about locally, and cycle repairs in Winton were an evening job for Bill Martin whose daytime job was driving a green Dennis wagon for Hastwells Grocers and Provin merchants, Kirkby Stephen along with Cherry Hayton as co-pilot. Nearly every night Bill would cycle home from Kirkby Stephen with new tyres or mud guards over his shoulder, having purchased them from one of three main cycle dealers. Namely, Waltons, Langhorns, or W Jacksons. It was every youngsters ambition to have a bicycle. The first thing you saved for when you left school and got a job - £3 19/6 bought a brand new bicycle. Either a Vindec Rayleigh Rudgewhitworth, Hercules, BSA and other makes, and it you weren't tall enough to reach the pedals, 2" wooden blocks were bolted on each side of the pedals. There was only the one size bike and you bought your bike for life; and the other ambition was to have made to measure a pair of Tom Broderick's corduroy knee britches, £1.25 (£1.5s, with strengthened knees and which you could have re-kneed when necessary. Tom Broderick, Titch Moffat and Judge Lawson were the three main Gent's Tailors in Kirkby Stephen for made to measure, or alterations to existing clothes.

The Ribble buses came through Winton on their Kirkby Stephen, Appleby, Penrith run. 10 to the hour into Kirkby Stephen and 1/4 past the hour back down the valley, and the fare was 2d from the square and 1d from the bottom road end into Kirkby Stephen. Watty Sayer, Herbert Braithwaite, Lol Spooner, Jack Edmondson, were drivers and conductors. They never refused a passenger, move up the alley and hold on to the rail was their cry when the bus was getting full.

Come early Spring, Bill Kipling, the 'mowdy' (mole) catcher came to life. Every evening Bill was out round the Parish, either setting traps or checking his traps and if he came across one which took a lot of extra time and traps to catch it was a 'misteched' one, Bill informed the farmer and that one counted as five when drawing his pay. Bill, during the day, was a gardener at Eden Place Mansion.

We can't forget Fred and his goats. Fred Allison lived in what was then the last cottage on the left going onto the Common. He had two small garths where he had small tin huts where he wintered maybe up to 20 goats. Every Spring Fred would 'kid' his goats and in full milk sell them to the hill farmers to go round with them when lambing so any weak lambs could have fresh warm milk. When the farmer was finished lambing he kept the goat for milk until it became a nuisance and Fred would either get them given or buy it back for little money. Finishing up tethered on the common and its breeding cycle starting again. Fred, through the day, was a linesman on the LNER at Kirkby Stephen and he had a small white pony which was heathed on the village green and village manorial waste.

Down the other end of the village lived Wilf Bousfield who farmed with his parents and sister. Besides farming, Wilf did quite a bit of sheep dealing. One regular order he had was every back end for 200 + black faced Wedder lambs to go into Derbyshire to be kept out on the open fell until 4th or 5th shear protecting fell rights. But us lads remembered him best for his all black dog , Sam, who did acrobatics. Hold your arms out to make a circle and Sam would jump through, plus Wilf had a 3 wheel Morgan car. You inserted the starting handle in the side between the front and rear wheels. It was always an education to watch Wilf start it. It generally got its full pedigree before he got it started. It was always kept on the roadside, his father wouldn't have it in the yard, it would; 'set all a fire!'

Another activity which happened every three or four years was when walking to Kirkby Stephen the back way, you noticed mostly giant Beech trees and some oak marked with a notch. You knew then Arthur Green from Silsden was coming to fell and remove those trees. How they felled those large trees: first letting them in all round with their large felling axes, and they made their own axe shafts out of young ash saplings and then with long cross cut saws sawed the trees down.

Sometimes with the use of ropes and two men to each end of the saw and with the use of wedges dropped it where they wanted it. When down they dressed the tree, leaving the main trunk as long as possible. After they had cut out the best, the rest was cut into approximate 6' lengths and put in a tidy heap, one heap for each tree. Next, providing the ground was dry, the horses and wagons came to remove the trunks to Kirkby Stephen LNER station. It was a sight to see. Sometimes 3 or 4 pair of mostly large shire horses per wagon. The only aids for lifting and loading were the set of 3 legs plus wire ropes, blocks and pulleys. Once to the station they were loaded onto low flat rail wagons. The other two estates where they also felled at the same time were Stobars Hall and Beck Foot. Altogether from the 3 estates maybe 40 trees in all. The last operation was selling the firewood, generally on a Saturday afternoon, by auction. Each heap was sold with the auctioneer standing against it, namely from 2 shillings to 7s 6d per heap to be removed by a certain date and all left tidy. It was mostly railway or quarry men who purchased the heaps for winter fuel.

Footpaths and Stiles - Stees

For its size, Winton was very well endowed with the above. The main village one 'Back Stees' starting at Winton House and nearly every dwelling on that side having access to it from their own back yards right up to the Common. In all 20 main in line stees, not counting any giving access from dwellings to it. Continuing from the Common you can still follow stees right up to the fell. Joining the bottom Fell Lane just below the railway line, another footpath starts at Ewbank House, which takes you to join Kirkbanks, 200 yds short of Eden Place Mansion. This footpath's name is 'Back Stees to Kirkby'.

Two thirds of the way on this footpath to Kirkby, there is a spur off to join up with Slack Gap Lane, very much used by local quarry men walking to work at Hartley Quarries.

One other much used path was to Kaber, starting with a stile, against the gate into the first pasture on Humriggs, opposite Hill Top, and coming out at the bottom of Kaber Village.

Another lane very much used was Peggy Lane. It was a lot kinder to your horses than Hill House Hill as Hill House was steeper, hard metalled and tarred.

One other very popular and very scenic footpath with stees was from Beck-A-Waden Bridge through to East Field Bridge, passing the picturesque Eden Tumbler Falls.

Briefly on Bridal Ways, there were many, but I think we had better let sleeping dogs lie.

Regarding the shops in Kirkby Stephen which you contacted the most: Gents Barbers - there were 3. Ernie Walker, Judge Lawson and Kerslakes. Haircut for 2d. There was only 1 style - short back and sides. Your sideboards trimmed with a dry cut throat razor, it made you cringe. Cobblers - 3 again. Yares, Jessops and Walkers. Clogs were the main type of footwear. Fish and Chip Shops - 3 again. Tattersals, Johnstones and one just above the Jolly Farmers Inn. 1 saddler Wilkinson, cafes; Fountain, and Armstrongs; Tobacconist, Simpsons; druggists, Browns; dentists; Elliotts, sweet shops; Elliotts, LAAL shop; North Road, and School Shop, plus others.

Looking back at village life in the 30s, you had fond memories of all the different seasonal products which became available as the year progressed and which you looked forward to. Be it from the local farms or local farmland, or from your own vegetable garden, every house had a veg garden and how good it produced, was how good your parents were at gardening, plus as you got older, how you took to gardening. The output of the garden was very much part of your staple diet as far as greens went. You must remember in those days there was no freezing of veg or meat, so as things came into season you looked forward to them. But as soon as their season was over, that was it until next year.

As regards the two fruiters who came round, they had a very limited selection. Here again very seasonal, nothing like as to what is available today. Plus the purchase of fruit was not very high in a working family's budget, therefore you were very dependent on your own garden, your farmer connections and your knowledge of the wildlife in your area.

Briefly, on setting the garden, all I can remember about setting it was, your number 1 job, you must have a load of farm manure and about half way through setting it you were detailed to walk into Kirkby Stephen and go to Harry Wilson's, Royal Arcade, and get the cauli and cabbage plants, generally a score of each. His small market garden was on the bank, down towards Melbecks and he used to grow them very rank in stitches. 'I suppose your father will want his usual?' and with a trowel he dug a clump out of each. No counting, wrapping them up in newspaper. 'That'll be 4d each, 8d in all. Is thee Father all right? Reet, well on thy way.' Harry was a man very sparse with his words.

Now as there was colder weather November-December, it was time for the first pig killing, and it was the rule always one before Christmas, as all the farms always killed at least two, and the married farm men and the retired farmers at least one, and there was great rivalry as to who had the biggest. It wasn't classed as a pig unless it was at least 24 stone and you had claims of up to 40 stones, but you could afford to brag as there was no way of weighing them!

So we will set the seasons off with pig meat, as this could be from early November to late March. Be it through your friends or farm work friends or near neighbour and as there was all the sausage, spare rib, black pudding, chine, crackling, brawn, liver, cheeks and trotters to be eaten within two to three weeks, so you can now see killing a pig was a very communal occasion. You could purchase any of the above from the pork butcher, but home made and for nowt tasted a lot better. Come Christmas, as regards your Christmas dinner, it was a very local affair. Turkey were unheard of, but certain poultry keepers in the village catered for the local need. The star was to have a goose, then an Aylesbury duck. If you couldn't afford an Aylesbury, a Kaki, Campbell. Among the cock chickens the cream was a Rhode Island Red or a Light Sussex, then it could be pheasant, guinea fowl or a roast of meat or a rabbit.

Another way to try to obtain your Christmas dinner was to go to the local whist drive. There was one every night somewhere local, starting late November. It was one way of raising funds for different good causes and the prizes were either live poultry or a bottle, and at Winton School on a whist drive night, the porch floor would be covered with geese, ducks, chickens and guinea fowl, alive all with their heads protruding out of a sack and nearer to Christmas it got and the professional who had not won his Christmas dinner was getting desperate and may the Lord be with you. If you happened to be his partner and you played a wrong card, come January/February it was a thin time of year. Maybe a good turnip rabbit, how the rabbits used to know where the turnip fields were, but they would travel a mile to one and they must have known that a turnip was not at its best until it had been frozen at least once.

So it was not until March/April with spring coming that hedge grown gooseberries came ready, only enough for a saucer pie for a start and the water cress from the beck, and by late April the rhubarb which was well cultivated and forced by using old buckets with their bottoms knocked out and again late April we used to walk the beck for that odd stray duck egg or two.

Again late April, the young crows were at their prime. As soon as they started to sit out of their nests, the local shooting men appeared. It was said that crow breasts pie was very good, but it was a dish that I never had the chance to taste. North Westmoreland had many rookeries. It was part of the every day scene having the crows around you.

In May/June your gardens were starting to produce first the shallots and late June who had to be the first with new potatoes and there was only one variety Arran Pilots, and the fishing season was now well under way. The local fishermen often had some trout to give away, how they had actually been caught, you didn't ask.

July/August - this was really the harvest time for most wild products. Wild strawberries, not so big but very sweet, wild raspberries also, and for those two products the railway embankments, they seemed to like the ash ballast.

Mushrooms - first the pasture ones and then the fog ones. Not a very consistent yearly cropper. Some years a glut, some years hardly any, and for the lady folk it was an all going on job for their flower and fruit wines and cordials, herb puddings, nettle beer, pickles, etc. and at the same time your cabbages, cauliflowers and other garden produce were now at their peak.

September/October - it was now the start of the rabitting season again. Although too many half grown ones from second and third litter were still a nuisance.

And where the wild 'cushacs' pigeons were a nuisance to the grain crops, it was a case for Tony Cleasby of Kirkby Stephen with his decoys, gun, dog and hide hurdles, and on a good afternoon bag 60 - 80.

It was also the peak time for the fruit harvest, brambles, crab apples, cooking and eating apples, but not many pears, plums or damsons.

One other ongoing product which was available all year round was the milk beasting for beasting Puddings. It had to be from the second milking of a newly calved cow and your farmer friend would say, 'Ask your Mother if she can do with some beasting'. With a sprinkling of nutmeg, it made a delicious pudding.

I think we have been round the year among the wild seasonal products, but we must not forget about the main farm crops, lambing time, hay time, harvest time and the potato and turnip crops, and on how good or bad these main harvests were governed everyone's man and beast style of living for the coming winter.

To conclude, you see that in the 30s, we lived a lot nearer to the land than we do now and I apologise for any products or seasonal things I have missed out.

Sayings and Doing amongst Live Stock and Farming

Be it a horse, beast or dog, when approaching it always talk to them especially if they haven't seen you coming. When leading any animal by halter or staff, always hold it with its head up high as any unruly animal has twice the neck power if it can get its head down low. When leading cattle or driving or leading a horse, make sure that if you had to part company suddenly that your hands are free to release the reins or halter. On no account any slip loops over your wrists. Always remember there has to be bad days, else you would never appreciate the good ones.

Popular Sayings of the 30s were:

1   If thou keeps owt wick remember it is liable to dee.
2   There has to be fools else the wise ones could nivver mak a living.
3   A rolling stone gathers no moss.
4   A man who bids is worth an awful lot of looker ons.
5   Nowts cheap unless you have a use for it.

6   We are often broke, but never broken.
7   If it is weel bought, it is half selt.

One thing that was drilled into you until they saw you were doing it correctly was whenever you took a horse, cow or stirk by halter into a field to release it, you always had to make sure you turned it round with its head to the gate before slipping its halter, as all animals can be a bit boisterous when newly released and their favourite manoeuvre was for head down, and a vicious double kick with both hind feet and the further you were from the firing line, the better.

What Niver?

That was the general expression when it came out that Miss Capstick was going to buy a brand new brick bungalow and then to let it off as an investment. 'Niver heard of owt like it. We've plenty of hooses as it is and of all things a bungalow'. But to stir things up further, she also decided to have two brick three bedroomed houses as well. The bungalow was on land between Mosscroft and Yew Tree House at the bottom of Hunger Rigg and the two houses on land attached to Sunnyside, the complete all told price for the bungalow, £250, and for the two houses, £300 each. To divide the portion of land for the two houses off from the rest of the field, a wall was built of more mortar than stones. The mortar was made of slecked lime and ashes and that was a new one for the locals. 'Nivver seen a warr built like that afore'. Miss Capstick was definitely very much part of Winton. On her sit up and beg Sunbeam cycle, complete with skirt guards and if raining, she rode with her umbrella up. She lodged with Mrs. King of Kings Terrace, but she also had another residence, fully furnished in High Street, Kirkby Stephen. Now in the early 30s wirelesses were just in their infancy. Not every household had one, so Miss Capstick used to visit houses in wintertime with her portable gramophone and records. The records I remember best were the Posthorn Gallop, Spring Time in the Rockies, and With My Gloves in My Hand and My Hat on one Side.

Now the time had come, 1938, to leave school and farming being the main employer for school leavers. As I was always keen on farming, it suited me. My first place for three half years was with W Coulthard, Cote Garth. But in more detail, Billy and his twin brothers and Mother had been farming Rookby Scarth and Cote Garth together as one farm. Cote Garth house had not been occupied for some years. On Billy's marriage the house was refurbished and Billy and his wife took over Cote Garth and I lived in at Cote Garth. But in the 1 and a half years I was with them, Cote Garth and Rookby Scarth were one unit for dipping, clipping, hay time, etc. I spent 50% of my time down at Rookby Scarth. The other staff at Rookby Scarth, along with Billy's twin brothers John and Robert was Joe Mooney, an Irishman who had settled down in the Kirkby Stephen area, perhaps 50 - 55 years old; and there was Mary Bousfield as servant girl, later to become Mrs. John Coulthard. Now Rookby Scarth had quite a big fell flock, Cote Garth not quite as big. Shorthorn cattle on both farms, but Rookby Scarth used to do some gisting in maybe 200 half bred hogs, and quite a lot of work horses. Any farmer in Winton or Kaber who wanted his horses out of the way for 1 or 2 weeks or longer up to Cow Close, Rookby Scarth. How they kept a record on how many weeks per horse was there, I wouldn't know. Rookby Scarth also used to buy 100 black faced wether hogs to summer and sell at the Autumn as shearlings.

Cote Garth

As sheep were the main enterprise on the farm, they got the most attention. As in those days Fell sheep lived off the fell. No hand feed, turnips, etc. Just a little hay in a very hard storm when they were completely frozen out. Even in winter the fell was their main pasture. Inside land was kept as clear as possible just to give them a clean bite after lambing. The only time a gimmer sheep was kept inside was for its first winter as a hog to build it up for its future life on the fell. So in the winter the weather glass (barometer) was read two or three times daily as the glass only had to start slipping and you knew a change was on the way. How much the glass kept slipping gave you an indicator of how strong the storm was going to be and the first move was to go and remove the big slate on the smoot hole in the fell wall giving the ewes access into high Langrigg allotment. They knew how stormy it was going to be and came down accordingly. And their Heath was Beales Fell just under the Nine Standards. There was also a stone fold on Beales Fell which we used to use mostly in the spring when the sheep was due to lamb on, and the due date we used to gather them

Brough Hill Fair -c1932

Hartley Coronation Festival 1911

Two local farmers checking over new strays in Hartley village pun fold

Winton School 1936

Pastoral Scene, near Winton

Winton Mill - c1906

Ready to set off to go milking to the High Ground 1933

Frankie's Great Uncle Jim 88 years of age

Tattie Scratting - c1935

Morris Oxford farm cart conversion c 1935

Team Work - Sweeping Hay - c1936

The author sitting with brother Ivan 1935

Pansy Marston, village May Day

Lance Metcalfe - Farmer, Howgill House

Cattle watering at communial beck

Winton & District Young Farmers 1939

Luke Fair, Kirkby Stephen early 1930's

Winton village

Horses waiting to be shod at Winton village smithy

Bay Horse Inn - c1937

Clydesdale Stag's untouched, Brough Hill Fair

all up into the fold and draw out the first week lambers and the same procedure the two following weeks. So that even in winter the fell was used to its upmost.

J Elwood, Winton Field, and his brother Alf at Row End, Warcop, used to send the 200 half bred Gimmer Hogs for summering. But their own men used to come up to clip and dip them. Now at Cote Garth there were 10 or 12 shorthorn cows and heifer replacements, plus rearing bullocks. The cows milked by hand, the milk separated for butter, churning day once a week and the blue milk fed alongside linseed gruel to all rearing calves up to 6 or 8 months old. Weaner pigs bought May or June to rear and fatten ready for the Autumn and next year's home cured bacon and ham. Nearly all farmers and farmmen purchased weaner pigs late Spring to rear and fatten ready for their next supply of bacon, etc. J Richardson, Windy Gate and J Waugh, Winton Hall, kept breeding sows and there was a ready market every Spring for their weaners. As they couldn't supply all their demand, J Milburn, Butcher, Church Brough used to bring so many weaners back every week late Spring from Darlington auction where he went weekly to purchase heavy pigs for his sausage trade, generally to order. One benefit I had when I started work was I had learned to milk, operate a separator and was used to handling some horses whilst going to A A's farm after school. If you had to be asked what sort of a boss Billy was, you could sum it up 'he could just about make summat out of nowt'. He was very versatile in so many ways, good stockman, horseman, waller, butcher, pig and sheep man, basic woodwork, it didn't matter what project undertaken, it was always a good strong sound job with what materials available. He was also in demand as a sturdy sheep doctor. His method was rather unorthodox but he was quite successful and it was a case the sheep would have died whatever happened. Another thing he was good at when working amongst mostly lambs and hogs, if one was not doing so well and looking a bit dried, he used to test it to see if it was not double scoped by giving it a sharp tap on its forehead with his knuckle of his index finger. If it gave a crack, that was it and the animal started to thrive, but I never mastered his technique as much as he tried to teach me.

As Cote Garth had been used as an off farm, a lot of the woodwork wanted attention. Doors, gates, partitions, etc. A lot of the inside field walls needed attention so if you weren't doing general farm work it was repair work. Riddling out walls and rebuilding them.

The biggest operation, even bigger than lambing, was hay time. The two farms roughly 100 acres or more of grass for hay. Billy and his brother John used to do all the cutting, with a pair of horses each. Billy always leading. All cutting to be done by 10 a.m. while the water was still on. Joe did all the hacking and raking off and Robert and I had to do the milking at each farm. All Cote Garth could be swept to the home barn and Crosser Field House, the same. Rookby Scarth 70% would be swept, either to Home Barn Field Houses or large Dutch Barn. Hay from the large Dutch Barn was carted home in winter, but in those days block carts with shelvings on you had 4'6" - 5' of dead cartage before you started loading your hay. As both farms were divided by the LNER from Darlington to Kirkby Stephen they both had 2 underpass bridges which restricted the height of your loads. The line from Rookby Scarth yard was approx. only 150yds away so railways was a part of their everyday life. Every Friday morning, the miners train came down on its way to the miners convalescent home at Silloth with new patients, returning late afternoon with rejuvenated patients. For sweeping if the hay and ground were in good fettle, the gate/wing sweep was used, but if just that bit off, tipping Tom sweep was used. With its prongs, it picked up that bit better. If the ground was wet, but the hay useful, out came the sledges. 3 horses with 3 sleds, 2 men loading them using hay rakes. Generally I was the in-between, taking and fetching. 1 man forking off and 1 man mooing and it was surprising how much ground could be cleared. Billy did all the sweeping with 2 fell ponies. He could stand on the back bar of the sweep. He and the horses were fully in charge as a team, generally at a nice trot, but sometimes he let them open up to a gallop. Now as the 2 farms were on the hill, the farmers in Winton and Kaber were finished hay sooner. They used to come up to help out. Generally bringing a young horse that wanted more handling. Alderman W J Dent, Kaber Fold, was up every day possible with his 4 wheel dray and a horse or two hitched on behind. We will just try this one in double chains. Perhaps one in the strawer, or siderake. He was a masterpiece with a horse. One day he landed up after dinner with a blood/hunter type behind his dray. It would be 17 hands, legs as long as giraffes with long prick ears. Now young man he said, this horse and you are going to get this horse raking caught up. So we yoked it into the horse rake, on the seat I got and he shouted, 'It's all yours'. Well, it was a good job we were in a big field. It took long raking trotting strides, it had no mouth, we were all over the place. I couldn't see where we were going, he was such a big horse. We must have been raking nearly a quarter of an hour before anyone could visualize what we were trying to do, but by nightfall both the horse and I had a better understanding of each other and Joe, the Irishman, christened it "elastic legs".

Now the night before Cowper Day, the yearly horse sale at Kirkby Stephen, privately in the streets, and always the day before Brough Hill Fair, Billy informed me that when I got up in the morning my breakfast would be ready and he would see to my morning jobs and I had to walk down to Kaber Fold, Kaber, to be there no later than 7.30 a.m. to give Alderman W J Dent a hand taking horses to Cowper Day. When I got there he was busy sorting them out. We put one in the dray, with 3 tied to the rear board of the dray and I led another 3 behind. We were in Kirkby Stephen before 9 a.m. and obtained the pitch he wanted, just above Hartley road end where we could park the dray and line up our horses for sale. Willy was well known in the horse trade and plenty of prospective customers eyed up the horses. Willy did the talking and I pulled out whichever one they were interested in and showed its paces up and down the street, 50yds up and 50yds back. You had to watch out, the streets were full of horses, all sizes and colours. Well, by 12.30 Willy said we have had a real good do, selling 6 horses. Here's half a crown, get something to eat, have a good afternoon looking around the fair, but be back at Cote Garth for milking. That half crown was real money, as I only had £10 for the half year. Just over a shilling a day. It wasn't that the farmer was mean, he had a struggle to make that money to pay you as times were still in the recession. Everybody, every trade or business was struggling to make a go of it. Myself, just I knew nothing different so we didn't consider it hardship, it was life.

Just 2 or 3 more memories of Cote Garth: one morning after breakfast, Billy said 'We have a big contract on. Go and bring Dinah in', one of the horses, a 2/3 year old, just broken in. Today we are going to collect a new horse cart and the set up was this special hill type cart had been made at Muker in Swaledale. It was a tub cart, ex car front axle and wheels and the shafts on the top of the kist right through to the heck. The axle was slung downwards, opposite to how it had been on the car and the axle clearance would be no more than 6" - a real fell side cart, the set up was. The joiner in Muker was bringing the cart half way and we were to meet him on the Nateby to Keld road at the Beck Meeting. So with our lunch, Dinah our fell pony, and a spade, we set off up the fell lane out onto Winton Fell. Across Hartley Fell Bottom, past Fell House into Birkett Allotment. Up to the top Hartley Fell gate, then following the fell wall up past the shooting box and then Duckerdell. Then heading for the road above Tail Bridge. Meeting our joiner on the road down to Beck Meeting. We sat and had our lunches, changed the horses round in the cart, stood back and looked to see if Dinah and the cart were compatible and then it was paid for - £15. So up to now things had gone very well, but we had problems on the Duckerdell stretch. It was only a foot trod behind the wall and we had to do detours onto the fell to get through but we made it back home.

Another seasonable time was getting in the sieves for bedding. Early September with a double horse mowing machine. Billy or John would mow platts of sieves in cow close allotment next to Winton Fell. Perhaps 5 or 6 acres. Left to dry for a week or two and then on a good drying day start sledding them back down to the 2 homesteads going onto the bedding lofts. They weren't too bad to load with a hay rake but forking them up into a forking hole was an art of its own.

Every back end there was so many lambs left over to winter as shotts. They were nicely wintered and by late spring and every week afterwards, one was slaughtered for the 2 farms meat supply and if it wasn't enough and there was clipping or dipping days with extra men - 2 that week.

Now hay bitting was a must every back end; First of all you had to make sure the hog house was ready. Properly cleaned out and all the racks around the walls checked for missing or broken staples. Water containers cleaned then the racks filled with the best sweetest meadow hay and then first your gimmer hogs were housed for 3 - 4 days or until they were eating the hay readily. This was done to make sure in early life that they ate it when offered it in stormy weather as hay was the only supplement for hill sheep. You always used a creel for taking hay to them and for bringing the wattings back home.

Early back end when there was more rabbits about, Billy used to smile and say, 'Tomorrow you are going game keeping.' Tim Walton a retired farmer who had farmed Grains-O-Beck Lunedale, and retired to Kirkby Stephen came for a day's rabbiting, bringing his ferret, nets, etc. A man of few words or action as long as his pipe was lit and it was my job purse netting the burrows for him. The only time he did raise his voice was when I had missed a pop/bolthole and a rabbit got away. Rabbits in summer time also lived in seats in the pastures. Pastures were not eaten bare as today. There was plenty of clumps of grass to make warm sunny seats and the farm dogs were for ever putting them up but the dogs soon learned that the rabbits were too fast for them.

My memory of pedigree shorthorn cattle was Foggathorpe. They were nearly all that prefix around Soulby and Kaber. W J Dent was a pedigree shorthorn man . In the early summer of 1938 W J brought a very large red blood coloured pedigree shorthorn bull plus some heifers up into Potts allotment next to Winton Fell and Winton Fell Lane. Now this bull had a bit of a reputation for being bad to handle so when he was turned out a small length of chain was left attached through his ring thinking it would be a big help when he was to be caught again. Well, he was a right crooner. Any person in sight or sound set him off and it was said that his own echo upset him more. So by early back end he was getting dangerous so he had to be brought in but that was more easily said than done. No one dare approach him with just a fell type wall between them so that next move was who had the best dog to hold a bull at bay. Well 2 or 3 tried but he was still the boss so the next I knew was that on the Sunday morning after we had bullocked up Billy told me to bring 2 horses in and gear them up for trace work and off we went with the 2 horses, 2 swingle trees and Thrib tree and a length of chain up to Potts Allotment. W J had been before us and being an ex military man he had disposed of the bull and it was our job to snig it down the fell lane to down under the railway creep to a waiting flat truck with a hand winch so that was the end of the Potts Allotment episode.

Two occasions stand out re Mrs. Coulthard, Cote Garth, who was a first class farmer's wife: one night, it must have been getting on towards midnight, and we were unloading our last load of hay on the loft at Rookby Scarth with the help of a lantern, when out of the darkness a voice said, 'Robinson, William, Come out here. If we are going to have to work to this hour of night to make our living, it is time to try something different.' When I appeared I was told in no uncertain terms to get up the fields to Cote Garth, get a wash and my supper was on the table. The other occasion was one wintery morning, Billy told me to take Dinah with Sled to fother the shearlings down the low pasture. What happened whilst I was putting the hay out in canches, I can't remember, but Dinah was off like a rocket for home - not through the proper gate but through a snicket gap. Just giving access to the next pasture for stock only. Well the sledge was wider than the snicket, so Dinah and it parted company, only the sledge was in pieces. I set off back to the farm wondering what sort of reception I would get and when I got near to the yard I could hear Mrs. Coulthard giving Billy a lecture re expecting too much, just a young lad, 14, and a young horse, newly broken, coming 3, so things turned out a lot better than expected.

Rookby Scarth

Three things stand out re Joe the Irishman: one was never ask him for a leg up onto a horse. He took great delight in putting you clean over, and one other was I was always 'boy' with Joe. This day he said, 'Boy, if you ever get detailed to take the coffee, tea or 6 o'clock can and basket back to Rookby Scarth, make sure if there is any Granny Loaf left, it doesn't make home. For Joe to have sight of it once, was enough. The other thing that amused Joe, was when the three brothers all turned out the same early summer morning in their kytle trousers and jackets. Joe used to say, 'Boy, I bet you can't tell which is the original masterpiece on any jacket or trousers.'

Well, as I had done 3 terms or one and a half years and my wages had gone up from £10 the first half year to £10 10s the second half year and to £14 for the third half year, my parents said I was worth £20 per half year. This was more than Billy could afford, so I went to the Martinmas hirings at Kirkby Stephen and was hired to James Cleasby, Hartleyfold for £19 the half year. This was a big farm. In those days milking 35 cows, wintering 160 head of cattle overall and a very prominent name in the shorthorn world. 500 black faced ewes to bred Masham lambs, plus 250 black faced fell ewes, plus hogs on Hartley Fell. The 3 years I was there the staff was static. James himself who was very prominent in public life being an Alderman and Magistrate and when he wasn't at meetings he worked full time on the farm. The Foreman was T Bousfield who had gone to the farm nightly and weekends from a very early age and he was a very keen stockman and more or less classed as a son as Mr. Cleasby only had 2 daughters. George High was the horseman but always referred to as Oscar who lived in Kirkby Stephen. Bill Bainbridge was the cowman and general worker who lived in a cottage in the main yard. J Dent was also single like myself and we lived in. For other labour there was Barney, the Irishman who came over every year mid June and he always brought a different brother with him and they stayed maybe for 2 months or more. There were 2 night men out of Kirkby Stephen for hay time and harvest, also to help in the farmhouse the first half year Eva Richardson and the following two and a half years, Ethel Donald.

Now as shorthorns were the number 1 breed in Westmoreland there was a lot of rivalry as to who had the best herd in the district. Not only topping prices and tickets in local auctions for newly calved cows, but also for types of breeding stock, cattle or sheep. All in north Westmoreland the Cleasby family were all noted stockmen. Three brothers: James, Hartleyfold; Tom, Grange Hall; and Bill, Gaythorne Hall and brother-in-law John Dent, Hartley Castle. Another brother-in-law, J Thompson, Green Rigg, they were all shorthorn cattle black faced ewes and Masham lamb men. So therefore stock rearing was the main enterprise on all these farms.

Back to Hartleyfold. The land stretched from the River Eden in Kirkby Stephen right through Hartley Parish to Langrigg Scarr and the Fell. The main meadow and the best pasture was between the river Eden and the homestead. Gradually climbing higher towards the fell. Most of the higher ground was 100% limestone. The main farm yard had the main road from Hartley to Kirkby Stephen with gates at each end going right through it. As dryness was a big problem among the ewes and lambs in summertime there was 360 acres of moss land on Stainmore, 7 miles away. Sievy Rigg Farm, 160 acres, they said was bought for £160. £1 per acre. Pattinsons Allotment 200 acres, rented from Helbeck Hall Estate and this land on Stainmore was made most use of in Summer.

With the war starting all farms had to alter their farming policies. Hartleyfold up to the war, the only ploughing they had was the same 2 acres for mangolds for the ewes and lambs, but the farm now had to grow roughly 20 odd acres of oats, 2 or 3 acres of potatoes, and 6 or 8 acres of turnips. So this was my real induction into arable farming But the emphasis was still 90% on stock farming. Horse power the first 2 years I was there was 4 Clydesdale horses, Turk, Jock, Sam and Betsy, plus one fell pony, 100% for riding only. Mainly for Tom who had an accident as a lad and walked with a limp. But at times when very busy among the sheep I seemed always to be gathering different lots and bringing them to the sheep fold for dipping, clipping, foot rot, etc. So I would have use of the pony, plus I was supplied with my own dog, Bess.

The other donkey was the Ford Model T Van which Tom always drove. A real workhorse. The window wipers you worked by hand from inside. (Every night after supper, 7 days a week Tom and I delivered milk around Kirkby Stephen, ladling it into jugs set outside the customers door, straight up and down Kirkby Stephen. There was no Crescent or West Garth Estates. The only diversion off the main street was Saur Pow and Mellbecks. All the village customers came to the farm to collect their milk.) The back axle used to whine always more noisily than the engine. 3 or 4 of us, plus dogs used to go Sievy Rigg for the day to wall and shepherd. And in hay time it was fitted with a Gelder Sweep and used for sweeping hay. But the third year I was there, a brand new Brown Ferguson TVO tractor, plough, stitcher and grubber was allocated and bought and it took over all ploughing work, hay sweeping, etc. Buildings were even altered for access to barns so that more sweeping could be done, but the horses were still used for lots of other work.

The van's other weekly job was to Kirkby Stephen every Monday with Tom, 2 x 17 gallon milk kits, copy and bucket; as Tom was the milker at the Monday newly calved auction, who partly milked all cows after they were sold to make them comfortable and see if they were correct. Tom's word was final in any dispute between buyers and sellers, re teat faults, light of quarters etc. I used to have to go with him on the Xmas show days early December when instead of say 25 was in, on the Xmas dairy show day there could be twice as many, and we milked them in turn as they came out of the ring. Tom would give me the wink and say he would milk the ones he knew were troublemakers, and he could handle them. The milk was brought back to the farm, and the wash house boiler fire was lit and the milk boiled, and then over the next 2 or 3 days mixed with gruel and fed to the stronger calves.

I was often at the auction, as in the spring every week there was one or two newly calved cows to sell, plus main lamb sales days, draught ewe sales, bullock sales, and clean cattle sales. Plus every back end 40 to 50 small cattle stores would be bought for wintering and summering. All the stock was walked to or from the auction. Whilst still talking about auctions, I said earlier that the Xmas dairy show was the big day, all the big dealers ambition was to win the Liverpool dairy show, so it was always planned to have 6 or more good cows calving down the week before to give you a chance. If lucky you may have 2 or 3 for the show, and it was in 1939/40 when new calved cow prices went barmy, always £26 was the limit for the very best, but they went up to £36 then £40. It was a bigger sensation amongst the farming community than Hitler, 2 years out of 3 we won the dairy show, just a slight touch of Ayrshire did the job, and one was sold that went on to win Liverpool, and came back home one week later to win Kirkby Stephen again the next year.

Whilst still talking about cattle, always 3 if not more young bulls were reared for sale every year, for sale, they had to be light Roan, with plenty of breeding behind them, and the received the best of everything, and were trained to halter and later staff, and nearly everyone had to wear wooden horn trainers. With buying 40 to 50 small stores every back end plus own reared bullocks, and non replacement heifers; Luke fair bullock day, and heifer day were both big days.

Now as regards housing all the cattle in winter; all except small calves were tied up, 7 byres at the homestead, and 7 field houses. With only 3 main cow byres having water bowls, all the rest had to be let out to water, either to beck or pond; so in winter from 6 a.m. to 9.30 a.m. it was milking and bullocking, starting again at night 3pm to 5.45pm. Milking was by machine, very heavy clumsy units, and were only used on those giving the most; Oscar, although the horseman, operated the milking machines and Tom and I milked by hand newly calved ones and others. James did all the calf feeding, and the other 2, Bill and John mucking out, feeding and watering etc. Milk was carried by hand at least 60 yards up out of the 2 main milk byres, out of the main yard, through the top yard, into the rear kitchen where the cooler was; when cooled churns had to be checked for correct measure, labels made out, and then rolled down to the milkstand on the main road. 17 gallon kits had just been replaced by modern 12 gallon kits. Hartley Castle and C. Harker, West View also used the same stand.

8 o'clock after breakfast, and 1 o'clock after lunch was when every man gathered at the bottom of the top yard for James to discuss and give you your main duties for that day; and everyone knew that if he had his cane stick over his arm things were in order; but if he was using the stick to mark out a type of pattern on the ground you got your orders and disappeared smartly.

In winter James, Tom, and myself had 2 field houses each, and what with all the sheep to fodder and shepherd, we were not available for general work apart from say 1pm to 3pm.

As hay was all loose, either in barn, dutch barn, or stack; cutting hay by hay spade or knife was an ongoing job, either for carrying in creels, or making into trusses or canches for taking out to the sheep. I would not know for sure, but it could have been the first farm in the area to purchase hay from 'ower top;' every winter a load was brought by Cheeseman of Rushyford on a white flat wagon, and it was cut and canched, but had been tied using a hand press, 2 to 3 ton no more. There was always a debate on its quality; Tom and James were always pulling each others leg on various subjects, and on one year Tom was examining a canch saying it was coarse rough stuff , off poor land, only fit for making chair bottoms; when James who had already inspected it said; 'now listen young man, you never grew good strong hay on bad land, and remember more men go broke by not buying hay than them buying it .'

Spring time was a very busy time; lambing 750 ewes, calving down the new crop of heifers, plus cows, as well as seed time. All lambing sheep had daily access to good quality hay from mid January onwards; 500 crossed ewes were lambed in the hills bottom, and when lambed moved daily to adjoining meadows where daily they were fed mangels, fingered by special horse drawn root cart. The 250 fell ewes were lambed up in the fat pasture before moving back up to the fell. The 3rd week of lambing was the most hectic as the crossed ewes were in their 3rd week, and the fell ewes in their 1st. By mid May the crossed ewes had been finished lambing by approx. 2 weeks so all the lambs were now considered ready for the long walk to Sievy Rigg/Patterson allotment 7 miles away as the crow flys. The night before approx. 450 ewes and 650 lambs plus so many shot hogs were all brought into Shade Hill pasture and outgang ready for a 3am start; James, Tom, and myself for the first 1 1/2 miles to be clear of Winton; after Winton James rode the pony back home, Tom having been riding up till then; the sheep knew the road, they knew where they were going, but I had to be up with the first hundred to keep them going ahead; if you got a stoppage with that number of sheep they took a lot of starting again, and even the Winton to Brough road was so narrow in places it had passing spaces. We reckoned that if we were at Brough by 6a.m. we had done all right; for after Brough clock it had been arranged before we set off which way we would be going; turn left down Brough, up the Helbeck road, past Helbeck Hall, and up past Thornthwaite farm into Patterson allotment. The other way; turn right at the clock, up Brough, to Lane Head farm, and then take the Middleton-in-Teesdale road to nearly Silver Well, and then across the gill to Sievy Rigg. After clear of Brough we used to let them take their time, hoping that many would get mothered up; so we used to sit by the roadside and have our breakfast, and by the time we had made our destination James would be there in the van as the next big job was making sure they were all correctly mothered up, before letting them out of sight. Sievy Rigg farm house was still in reasonable condition, and the garth was always kept well walled as we used it for clipping etc. Every 4th or 5th day was a Sievy Rigg day to shepherd and wall etc., and in hay time and if the weather was good it was a Sunday morning job but just to shepherd. By late august it was time to bring them back again for the early September lamb sales, going up early afternoon, and gathering them up into a small allotment at the Thornthwaite end of Patterson allotment, starting off the next morning again at 3 a.m. with James taking us in the van with Tom and myself walking them home. With the change of vegetation on the allotment you couldn't visualize how well both the lambs and the ewes had done, Tom used to say 'All tell thee wat Robin-a-Bobbin, now those are swelky lambs. We can do Kirkby', eyeing them over when gathered. Getting the lambs ready for the lamb sale, first they were spained and dipped, and then separated into gimmers and wethers, and 3 days before the sale they all had their faces washed in soapy water, and then clean water, and any a bit muffy, it was a careful plucking job. Then the debate started, gimmers first, the 40 best would be caught in a pen, and after careful appraisal the 20 best were the top pen, maybe another 4 or 5 pens of 20 to follow much the same, and then maybe a pen of Dunnies or a strong pen but not quite as good of skin or fleece; a bit dog haired Tom would say; and so on until all marketable lambs were selected penwise. The same procedure was done with the wethers and every pen was given a colour code, either on the ear, shoulder, neck, mid back, or rump; using coloured marking sticks, and all gimmers had their forehead tassel marked red as an extra identification.

Whilst still on the subject of sheep; the 3 married men, John, and I were, as a perk were allowed to buy a swaledale tup lamb each autumn which was wintered and summered free of charge, to sell as a tup shearling; if you gave up to 25 bob for a lamb it was pricey, and if one got 55 bob as a shearling you had done well. In those days 30 bob seemed to be the limit for an awful lot of shearlings and aged tups. Tom also had 3 ewes of his own and he never had less than 6 lambs and he always topped the market at £2 3s.

Another thing after hay time, all the meadows approx. 70 odd acres below the homestead had pretty deep drainage gutters bordering on one side of all the hedges and these were all fenced off with one strand of barbed wire, it being put up after hay time, and taken down when the meadows were freed. Every length of wire when rolled up was labelled with name of gutter and field. This was to keep the gutters from being trodden in by the cattle when they grazed the fog.

Now on ploughing and harvesting these were operations I had not had much experience on, and as Oscar was the horseman who did all the ploughing, stitching, bindering etc.; my main job was taking a pair of horses seed harrowing, and stitch harrowing turnips and potatoes with one horse. On seed harrowing lea....?.... I was told that you must never cross harrow until you had at least harrowed it three times straight up and down as ploughed. This is to make sure you got some tilth between the furrows to hold the seed from dropping through between the furrows. There was no seed drills, only a fiddle drill or finger and thumb. Now for turnips the ground was all made up ready, and then stitched and sown in platts approx. one third or quarter of the full area for turnips at 5 day intervals; this spread the hoeing out, giving you the chance to get them all hoed at the right size. As regard stitching up for turnips and potatoes, this is a very exacting job, stitches dead straight, no dog legs. It was every horseman's pride to make an eye-catching job. When harvest time came it was all 'haver' oats, barley was unheard of and with the land having been down to grass for years unknown there was tremendous crops, mostly all going down and some hard work getting the horse binder to handle it. On stooking, you were told always make your stook north to south so that they get the full benefit of the sun on both sides and the sayings were 'Never dream of starting to lead until it had seen at least 2 Sundays and been restooked once'. Better still it needed one good soaking to drive out the sap and when ready to lead 2 of you went ahead to butt-welt, always putting your butts facing into the sun and wind and as it was an additional crop to usual cropping it had to all be put into stacks and it was a work of art or good luck putting the prop in the right place. It was when the stack settled overnight that the truth came out.

Turnips

Actually sowing the turnips was an after supper job. Generally the boss or horseman and the horse with the smallest feet sowing in the late evening and with the evening dew coming down it was a help in striking the seeds. Turnip fly was a big nuisance, often crops having to be resown. But with staggered sowing you did stand a better chance and a farm with only a small plot of turnips with turnip fly and with a rag soaked in paraffin trailed along the top of the stitches helped. Harvesting the turnips generally started the third week in October, snagged by hand, topped and tailed, each man took two stitches at a time - two stitches to the right, two to the left, making a row of turnips. With heaps of tops in the same row every four or five yards. Therefore when you had snagged 8 stitches you had two rows of crop, just the right width between for your horse and cart. Firstly, you loaded up the tops and these were carted out to young stock still lying out as a supplementary feed and on odd days when you had no turnip tops available you gave them a load of tops and tail turnips and then the turnips were either carted home ready for winter feeding or pied in the field. Covered first, mostly with hedge slashings and then soil for later use. The object of growing a crop of turnips was not only as a supplementary winter feed but also to put some management back into the land. This was done by feeding sheep either for fattening sheep or breeding sheep and it was a general rule to leave four stitches on and 8 stitches to lead off. But you could use any permutation of your own, say 8 on, 8 off, but the least number was 8 if carting off to fit in with your horse and cart. Once you had cleared 8 stitches you could fence your break and let your sheep on and on the management side you didn't see until the next crop, rigging up, oats undersown with grass seeds and you could easily see how folding sheep produced such bountiful crops. Re fencing for sheep breaks, a light self grown conifer type round post was used with a nail near the top of the post slanting upwards and another nail to be just above ground level slanting downward for hooking on the wire. The wire used was approx 3 inch mesh, sheep netting and with the posts approx. 7 or 8 yards apart and 2 men with a mell and gavelot could soon remove and fence a new break. But if it was very hard frost and you couldn't move your fence, it was a bouncing job. With a crowbar you struck the side of the turnip and it bounced out, so that you could throw the turnip top and tail over to your sheep.

Other memories of Hartleyfold were getting cattle ready for sale. Special white sawdust from the sawmill, plenty of warm water, always finishing by first taking off all the water using a barrel hoop, then finally drying by rubbing sawdust in and then brushing it out by curry and brush and on the horns a nice rub down with wire pad and then rubbed with oil. And if a bit too cocky horned, up to an inch off with the hacksaw and then filed and sandpapered to make the blunt looking end respectable. And you knew no more than 1" off or you were into the wick and trouble. Halters had to be the plaited white type and it was the rule you sold the halter with the animal and there was a store in the top yard for halters, brushes, shovels and gripes. As every byre and field house had its own brush and shovel there had to be a store. James was a stickler for tidiness at all levels but it was a good education.

Now it is not everyone who has carted snow. The three years I was there were all good summers but hard winters and every storm the top yard next to the house filled with snow, so on the 3rd or 4th day when things were getting back to normal and all sheep accounted for, right lads just clean the top yard out. So with just one horse and cart and 3 or 4 of us we would cart 8 or 10 loads and tip it in the garth.

One other incident I remember, Tom and I were going to scale muck after lunch and walking out of the main yard we noticed a horse standing at the bull copy corner, harnessed and a part shaft attached. Tom said, 'Ha, somebody has been having fun' and we continued walking down the road. As we got to coffin bridge, who was coming up the road, but Jim Bracewell, puffing and blowing, he shouted, Have you seen a horse with its harness on', and Tom told him where it was. Jim then, with a big sigh of relief shouted, ' I knew it was bount to stop somewhere'. Jim was a local carter, mostly among coals, operating from the Low Station always with a 4 wheel dray.

Two jobs no one was allowed to do were operating the straw chopper or the grain crusher. These were exclusively James's territory. The chopped straw along with sawdust and moss litter were the bedding for all young calves.

Still on Hartleyfold, every Sunday morning was clean smock day. Everyone had to wear a khaki smocks when bullocking or milking and at 6 o'clock every morning, 7 days a week, James would bring down to the main yard, 5 mugs of hot tea. Everyone used to keep an eye open for him coming and as regards wages, the first half year I had £19, but for the 6th half year I was there it was up to £26.

Hartley Low Mill

Hartley Low Mill was really on the Eden on the road out of Kirkby Stephen to Hartley and in those days a very busy mill. Tommy Longstaff, his wife and daughter worked full time only getting an ease up in the summer. He not only ground but rolled and dried over a small kiln. His special operation was grinding and drying oats into Sussex ground oats. You would never dream of killing a pig if it hadn't consumed 1 cwt of sussex ground oats to make the leaves of lard firm and white. All the grain into and out was by horse and block cart and payment was by so much per bag. The same as for threshing, but this was abused by using bigger and bigger sacks, so the millers started to make a charge of so much per 1 cwt. and the threshing outfits so much per hour, plus free coal to thresh with and enough coal to get them to the next set up.

Three jobs on farms considered a doddle were either going to the corn mill or taking a horse to be shod, more so if it was new shoes all around, and the other was going to the station for a load of coals. Still on Low Hartley Corn Mill, the water for power was taken off Hartley Beck about 70 yards up Hartley Road. The Mill race and the water holding pond are both now filled in. Right next to the corn mill which was also adjoining the river Eden was the saw mill on the opposite side, lower down the Eden. But the remains of the Weir for diverting the water from the Eden to turn the sawmill can still be seen and it attracted many viewers every autumn to watch the salmon leaping to get up and over the weir. The weir, mills, mill race, and pond in those days were very much part of Kirkby Stephen scenery.

Re the supply of water to run both mills, the weather played a big part and the rule was as long as there was a head of water to turn the wheels, grinding and sawing was the number 1 priority. They never knew when a dry spell could restrict their work but after 1936, when Johnson and Philip brought electric to the area, they both had electric motors installed to switch over to when water was scarce.

General

General everyday topics were farming and more farming and weather. Football and cricket as of today unheard of. But Tom and Oscar used to have a small flutter on the horses. In those days there was no official betting slips, they just wrote the bet on an old envelope or any other sheet or piece of paper and the bet would be maybe sixpence each way double on two named horses, with underneath ATC, and another sixpence each way double giving two named horses. you see in those days to be an optimist, was a big help in life. ATC stood for any to come. James used to pull their leg, if only they could get their bookie to pay out on the also ran! And at times Tom would wind up Oscar and Bill to talk about the large farms they had worked on. Oscar's number 1 was when he was bullocky at Low Barn in Winter. He was bullocky up to 160 feeding cattle, all tied up, turnips ad lib for feed and water, rolled haver, seed grass, hay and haver straw. By mid December 10 - 12 going out fat every week. Then up to the end of February the same number coming in every week. By lunchtime he had been once round and after lunch he started off round again.

Oscar had also worked for 'Bool Ooot'. Bool Out was remembered by his Monday morning chorus. He was at the bottom of the hired lads stairs. By 5.30 a.m. hitting the stairs with his stick shouting, 'Bool Oot, Bool Oot, the day after tomorrow is Wednesday and that's half a week gone and nowt done, bool oot!'

Bill had worked in the West Cumberland area around Dearham, Black Hill and Cleator Moor. One place the Calf Garth was 32 acres and the front meadow 90 acres. Our black faced ewes were just rabbits to the size of sheep he had shepherded. I think a pinch of salt was required to digest some of these stories, but I'm not sure.

All the sevens

In winter one nearly full time job was muck leading and scaling muck. Oscar, as horseman it was his priority job; 7 field houses and 2 large midden steads at home to keep clear and it was often called all the sevens. 7 heaps of muck per cartload, although when the bow shafted cart came into being, the payload was increased to 9. 7 good steps between each heap, 7 good steps between each row. The first row 7 steps from the hedge. At the last heap from your cart you carried a marker on your drag rake, 7 steps to your right to give you guidance on your next row. It was a farmer's pride in seeing that the field of muck was set out with precision.

Now as regards predicting the weather it was an ongoing daily job, especially in hay time and harvest time. As there were very few wirelesses about, the weather glass which was nearly always hung on the wall adjacent to the back door, was the main instrument for predicting weather changes. It was never so far wrong. The main thing was you had to check it every 3 or 4 hours by giving it a light tap to keep it up to date. There were sayings you still hear today, Rain before 7, fine by 11, but one which was nearly always correct was, 'If there was a heavy watter (dew) on first thing, you could plan it to be fine, but if there was no 'watter' on, look out the day would worsen'. It was surprising if there was a field of hay gaily dry and the boss debating should we row it up and cock it. Hoping for a good day tomorrow, just to give it that final benefit. It just had to come 3 or 4 drops of rain in the wind and the decision was get moving it, it was ower good hay to miss.

Referring back to Hartleyfold, it is now no longer farmed as one unit and very doubtful that it will ever be so again.

So just for posterity, here are the names of every field on what was called Hartley Fold Farm, all then owned by J Cleasby but where rented will be marked with RTD:

Calf Garth, Far Calf Garth, Plantation, Granny Croft, Larches, Hills Bottom, Bull Copy, Corn Close, Rough Bottom, Millfield, Big Bottom, Ellers, Laalmires, Big Mires, 30 Yackers, Mason Mires (rtd), Mason Planting (rtd), Out Gang, Box Tree (rtd), Robertson Land, Hanson Land, Shade Hill Pastures, Lockhows under Line, Lockhows above Line, Shade Hill Meadow, Fat Pasture, New Close Under Line, New Close Meadow, New Close above Line, Celandine's Wood, Low Langrigg, High Langrigg, Fell House Meadow, and on North Stainmore, Sievy Rigg Farm and Pattersons Allotment (rtd). There was another out gang to the higher land by using Whingill Lane, then through the first gate on the right after West View Field House, through the narrow field into Fat Pasture, and there was one cattle creep dividing high and low lockhows and two high and low new close pastures and one level crossing between fat pasture and Celandine's Wood.

Hartley Fold Farm

In the 3 years I was there I can never recollect any professional veterinary surgeon visiting the farm. There was once we had a cow that put its calf bed out and Tom went in the Model T Ford van to Argyll House, South Stainmore, to ask John Willy Davies, the local cow doctor, who farmed there, to come and attend to it, which he did and the cow went on all right. The only other occasion was with Ministry men for an experiment on dosing lambs for worms. They selected and weighed 160 lambs and then put them into lots of 40, each lot with a different conspicuous mark. One lot was the control group, which received nothing, groups 2, 3 and 4 received different liquid drenches. 1 which if I remember rightly was a red brimstone mixture. They were dosed again at 6 weeks and at 12 weeks weighed again and comparisons made. I can't remember what the end results were.

7 by 7

Another skilled job was mucking the potato stitch prior to planting. It was a question of keeping your balance standing on a load of muck, putting a forkful of muck off the cart in rhythm. So that when it came to scale up the stitch it was evenly spaced. I always remember the first time I had to do that job. Oscar the horseman said I will give you a tip, concentrate on keeping your balance and if you haven't made a good enough job do the same stitch coming back and don't shout at all your horse will be waiting for any excuse to stop as it is hard work and a sudden unexpected stop is not on the books.

Another time the 7 by 7 system was used was in applying lime; with the war starting and the government starting to help financially, and the only lime being available was clot lime. Kibbled lime, ground limestone and residue of lime didn't come on the market in our area until later.

Hartley Quarries was right on our doorstep mostly turning out two trainloads of graded raw limestone per day for the steel works at Consett. But so much of clot lime was also produced to go out by rail and delivery by five ton lorry, locally to farmers and builders. Every builder and larger farmer had a lime pit for slecking it in and everyone knew where in the village you could buy a bucket of slecked lime, pure white; and not only farms but cottages as well used whitewash. So it was a terrific order when James ordered 50 tons, 10 lorry loads. With a gap opened in the wall between Hell Gill How and Lock How the loads were tipped out around the pasture. The same open tipper wagon was also used for collecting and returning the workmen from surrounding villages. Now as soon as the lime had started to fall, but before the sticky stage, Oscar and John carted it out into heaps, the same as for muck. It was Bill and I who had to scale it. The main thing was to keep as cool as possible. If your wrists or forehead started to sweat, the dust soon burned and made them sore.

Kirkby Stephen Workhouse

Another regular tradesman coming around Winton every other Tuesday in Winter were the two men with their horse and flat cart from the workhouse. Loaded with bundles of kindling, calling at their regular customers. I think the people only bought from them as a gesture to help the workhouse. In summertime the horse they used, used to go to Hartley to Kitty Harker's farm for a well-earned rest. Nearly every night there would be tramps coming into Kirkby Stephen for the night at the workhouse from 4 main directions: Sedbergh, Hawes, Appleby and Stainmore. They had to do so much work the next morning and chopping kindling was one of them and they were always referred to as milestone inspectors.

Hartley Fold Farm water supplies

Hartley Fold Farm was responsible for supplying Hartley Village water supply before the regional water schemes. Brunskill and Nicholson of Kirkby Stephen were the plumbers when any bursts needed repairing. Arthur Morland, the Clerk in charge of the Goods Depot at the Low Station, was the water rate collector. Twice a year it was his Saturday afternoon job.

Another farm that Hartley Fold supplied with water was Cote Garth from a spring in High Langrigg allotment.

Characters

Another character out of Kirkby Stephen was an elderly man called Mr. Warwick who used to come out to Winton and Hartley and scale muck for 2 or 3 farmers and the going rate was 4d per score. But he soon told them if the heaps were larger than normal and that bit too far apart. He always went by the name of Lightning.

One local character was John Shadwick, Hellbeck Grange, Brough. Every Monday morning playtime, quarter to 11 to 11 o'clock you could hear John's horse and float going past Wind's End on their journey to Kirkby Stephen market. It was a biggish horse, really too big for the float, but as John was a ploughing man it had to be a dual purpose horse and it had a gait more like a slither, nothing as precise as a clip clop. John's main wares were potatoes, butter, eggs, and rabbits. Never missing a Monday whatever the weather. It was said that in summer when he had no potatoes or rabbits he used to take bunches of mint. He was very much a man of Monday's market and well known with his 3 sons as an astute farmer. He was maybe better known by us lads for some of his sayings. On one spring day Calfy Willy from Russendal was up at his farm and had purchased 5 or 6 calves from him, 30 bob for the lot. They must have been slinkies and Calfy Willy said on paying him, 'How about a bit of luck' and John after a bit of thought said, ' Thou willt have to come back at the back end and catch tha sel a rabbit and Calfy Willy replied, 'And I suppose it will have to be yan that hasn't got a white tail'.

The other incident was on a threshing day at Hellbeck Grange. All neighbouring farmers used to join for threshing and up to 10 extra men were required to operate a threshing set. One cutting bands, 1 feeding the thresher, 2 forking sheaves to the thresher, 2 keeping the bottling end clear by making a stack or loading onto carts, 2 looking after bagging the grain and carting it away, 1 looking after the chaff and the threshing operator keeping up steam. So in general 10 extra men for dinner and on this day, as all the men came out from dinner, John was standing outside the back door and exclaimed, 'How was the dinner lads?' and they all replied, 'Verra good' and John remarked, 'And verra good, that's the last of the old billy goat'. In North Westmoreland dinner time was 12 o'clock precise. Lunch was unheard of in the farming community.

Our 2 most local stonemasons lived in the village. Jack Farrer was one and he also kept 2 or 3 cattle. His land was the last enclosed land from Winton Common to the first Fell Common Gate. His workmate was Willy Sanderson. It was a regular sight every morning, just after 7, and back again just before 6, to see them on Shanks' pony to or from their work which could be up to 5 miles away. No cement mixer, just a walling hammer, trowel and shovel. As breeze blocks were unheard of and bricks still in their infancy. It was just local stone and mortar. For the mortar, it was slecked lime and beck sand. Depending on the size of the job, be it a new byre attached to a barn, or rebuilding a gable end, there had to be the stone, slecked lime and sand ready for the job. For the lime, if the job was big enough, a pit had to be dug to hold a cartload of cob lime from Hartley quarries which was then slecked ready. For sand, it was either down to the Eden at Linehams or Lady Ing Gravel Beds. A lot of gravel was carted out every year for cart farm track maintenance. It was surprising how every flood kept replenishing the sand and gravel beds. A must for shovelling gravel or sand was a round mouthed shovel. Whether all householders and farms had right to gravel and sand from the Eden, I don't know, but I think they must have had. Years later, when on moving to Nateby, I got 5 loads of gravel from the Eden at Watter 'Yat Bottom and John Hird of Castlethwaite said he was in charge of the Eden and I had to pay him 1s per load. But Matthew Robinson of Low Farm, Nateby, queried it as any person paying rates in Nateby Parish was allowed access to the Eden and to further Matthew's case, Watter 'Yat is in Nateby Parish, not Mallerstang. But on this, I think you had to ascertain on which side of the Eden you were. Jack and Willy both had the same garb: heavy corduroy trousers with straps below the knee to take the weight off and navy serge tunic/jackets which buttoned up to the neck, quite long and liberal pockets. This type of jacket was often the garb of the old horse dealers and the gypsy fraternity.

Now what about the local hedges and walls. From the village to the fell it was all limestone walls and you were taught that when repairing gaps, make sure to riddle out until you have a good solid base to start rebuilding on. Snouts slightly up to make it water shot, all joints crossed and keep your middles well filled. When you have learned the art you eye the stone you require next, pick it up and a good waller never throws one back.. With limestone you always have to be on the lookout for good top stones to finish off your gap and good throughs among limestone are rare. My opinion is that if you can wall limestone, you can wall owt! But singling a limestone gap tried your patience.

Hedges were all down on the better land and nearly all grown on a cam and ditched at one side and if the ditch was on your side it was your neighbours hedge.

In the Winton Hartley area, keeping hedges good was an uphill job. With being grown on a cam, they droughted sooner and rabbits riddled the cams with their burrows. In the 30s your hedge could be made of a good regular laid thorn hedge, but with the recession, many had grown too high, gone wild, died and left gaps. These gaps were the problem. The only way at first was to dry hedge them. That is utilizing the longest spare thorns from when re-laying hedges and also using posts, also from re-laying waste. First of all, from out of re-laying waste you selected the best long thorns and then selected any wood which would make posts. Nearly all hedges had some ash or hazel mixed in and these were your source for posts. Cut into 4 and a half feet lengths by cross cut, they were then split by metal wedges into semis, quarters or more, depending on the size of the trunk and then sharpened ready for driving in to keep your long thorns in position in the gap. If the boss said you were going thorn stobbing today, you understood. All neighbouring farmers in winter would be hedge laying. If you had more good thorns than you required, before burning them, you offered them to your neighbour and leading thorns on a cart with shelvings on was another art to master. When you got your hedge laid and gaps stobbed up it looked quite a good job, until the live hedge burst into leaf, plus your dry thorns soon dried out and collapsed and nearly every year you had to re-stobb. Now the last job left after hedge re-laying was to clean up and nearly everything finished up on the stick heap. Anything that would make firewood logs, oven sticks, or kindling all came home. Every farm had a stick heap and 'Hag Clog,' and any thorns loft or rubbish were burned in the field. Your tackle for hedging was a good medium axe, leather mittens, slasher, mell, cross cut saw, one cutting wedge, two drifting wedges, sledgehammer and lastly but very importantly, your wet stone. As in those days you were the most mechanical thing on the farm after the horse and if you kept your tools sharp and in good nick it made labouring easier and the grind stone was a much used piece and as lads, you were often roped in to turn the handle.

The next stage re hedging was the rail and post era. First, the big estates who had abundant trees to fell or thin out sent the trunks to the local sawmill to be cut into either 9' or 12' rail bars and posts into 5' lengths. The very best was oak, then larch, then ash, in that order. Here again when erecting a post and rail fence it had to be a good eye-catching job.

Another type of fencing for where you had to keep the price down was where you had to buy slab wood, reject lengths of wood from the saw mill with no more potential left in it. These were used as rail bars and posts but very subject to wind and hence a limited life.

Another use from out of the surplus thorns when hedge laying was to take 6 or 8 good straight bushy thorns which you threaded through a field gate with the bushy ends protruding from the bottom of the gate and with 2 cow bands for coupling the gate to your horse traces, you had your own home made chain harrows. It made a very good job, you just had to catch the muck at the crumbly stage. Also on hedges, when splitting for posts or logs always split down the grain, never up. Nearly every farm of any size had a corner fenced off which had been planted with larch trees; not many, 10 - 20, and these were your wood bank when required for new gates, roofing beams, boards, etc. Rail bar fencing was just starting to take its cycle in the hedging era. The local sawmill was the venue for getting it sawed into whatever you required. I was told that before my time the local joiner called Lambert, had his joiner's shop up Mellwood Yard, Winton, and his saw pit was on the village green right opposite Mellwood Yard Gate.

The next era in fences and hedges was as it is now, the wire fence. Firstly the fence made up of 6 or 7 long wires, nailed to posts at precise intervals, but soon taken over by the ideal fence of today.

One of the first changes as from horses to tractors was the bow shafted cart. In the late 30s you were going modern by changing the hooped wooden wheels on your best cart to ex lorry wheels and axles. Both the front and rear axles were used and with the broader tyres than the iron hooped wheels you could get on the land sooner. But with lowering the cart 9" your horse was not in proportion so to balance the job you had fitted bow shafts with a 9" bow or bend in them. These had to be of ash and steam bowed to make the job right. Deeper sides and end boards were fitted. You were a cut above the other lads with the new type cart. I remember an old farmer saying to his hired lad, 'Why do you always take the rubber tyred cart?' and his reply was that is was a lot quieter and the old farmer replied that when he was a carter, there was nothing he liked better than a cart with a good naf, the naf being the noise tap tap like which the wheels gave out, with naf naf anywhere from ¼ to 1" side movement on the axle.

Sledges

In winter when fothering the fell sheep in hard weather it was always by horse and sledge and the main thing to watch out for was on ground sloping downwards when frosty and snow covered was the sledge running on its own into your horses heels which upset most horses. So you always carried 2 cow bands with you to slip under the sledge runners to act as brakes.

Railways/Demurrage

As railways were the number one transport in and out of Kirkby Stephen, demurrage was a major cash controversy and the railways had a strict rule on the time a customer had to clear any wagons consigned to him. I am not sure but I think it was 2 clear days working from time of notification of arrival, then strictly x shillings per day or part of a day. As telephones were still in their infancy, notification of arrival would be by telegram which, being time stamped, settled any disputes on time of notification. Those telegram lads in their uniforms and on their regulation bicycles, really earned their wages. It didn't matter what the weather was like, they had to deliver the telegrams.

One story told about demurrage was about the station master who had too many pals amongst the farmers and local businessmen and he was very lax re charging and collecting demurrage. One back end he was off work for over a month through illness and a relief station master took over. The demurrage he charged and collected was considerable. Well, about a month later after he came back to work the station master was visited by a senior official who asked him to explain why when he was in charge hardly any demurrage had been collected and when a relief took over, it was just the opposite. Scratching his head and thinking fast, he said, 'It's like this, when I'm in charge all the locals who have known me for years know damned well I stand for no nonsense and make sure their wagons are cleared in time!'

It's a Wind Up

Well, first of all, what is a 'wind up'? Looking back to the 30s when wirelesses were just in their infancy and TVs unheard of, people had to make their own everyday entertainment to break the monotony and there were many ways. And one more so in those days than now was 'a wind up job'. First you had to have a character and you must be well aware of his or her strong feelings on a certain subject, be it politics, pride in their work or hobby, nature, plus many more. Living in a village everybody used to think they knew all about everyone else. The most likely time to set a wind up job was when you and your fellow workers/pals were going to sit down for a meal. Be it in a hay, harvest, turnip or potato field or the provin house which was always used for outside meals but it could also be on the village square after work. Someone would give you the wire who it was going to be wound up. Don't rush it, wait till we are well through our bait and it could go two ways: one to build their ego up re their pet subject/obsession or else to contradict on whatever they said. It was surprising how long a wind up could last. The more of you who twigged on what was going on, also gave a hand. At odd times it finished with the character never seeing through it, but generally it finished by the character twigging on, exclaiming 'You B.....s! It's a wind up!' At the same time you had to be on your mark to make sure that you won't the one for the wind up. Nobody was immune.

Brough Hill Fair

Another main interest at the fair was the cheap jacks who not only amused you but also conned you or worse still, their confederates picked your pockets. To get a crowd around them, was by one standing on a box shouting and displaying his wares, say favourite items being pocket watches and also as the crowd gathered he would be throwing and giving away pencils, anything to get a good crowd. Then he would give his spiel about his wares. 'What a bargain, which could never be repeated at that price! Unless he went out and stole some. And remember Ladies and Gentlemen, you are dealing with the most reputable firm in the North of England. We are not here today and gone tomorrow. No, we will be gone tonight!' After starting his watches off at 10 bob and in the next breath saying he wouldn't rob you, he would be down to 8 bob. Then 6 bob. But finally at an offer no person could refuse, 3s/6d was his bottom price. Put your hands up who wants one. With 3 or 4 of his mates in the crowd buying, he soon had a good sale going. Then out of sight for an hour, then the same procedure at the other end of the fair.

Another big crowd puller was some of the boys falling out with each other. After much shouting it generally finished up with them bare fist fighting, no holds barred. The police only gave them 2 or 3 minutes and then stepped in before each family joined in. Some family feuds went on from fair to fair.

Long Pastures

Winton was well blessed with long pastures as the village was like the hub of a wheel and all the roads and lanes out of the village made the spokes and at the spring of the year and when fodder was scarce, and as soon as there was any grass on the road sides, farmers vied on who grazed which lanes. Low Merricks Lane, Merricks Hill Lane, East Field Lane, Tarns Lane, Gull Slack Lane, and Mattock Lane could be grazed by barring 2 or 3 stirks or a horse in with a pole across, but as there was no water available it was only for 3 or 4 hours at a time. The other road most vied for was over the common. There was an unwritten law on who grazed the common and looks would have been enough. If you owned an animal caught grazing on the common, who by the unwritten law was not allowed to.

The other more used roads, Hartley, Kirk Banks, Beckawaden, Kaber Cross, and Lady-ing were grazed by personal herding cattle going out daily to their pastures, and Hartley, Kirk Banks, Over the Common and Appleby Lane still had grass centres for the horses.

Winton

The person who all the villagers looked to as the squire, was RR Sowerby, Winton House. He farmed it with 2 full time men. He was also a solicitor but not in active practice. But he was always there to help anyone who had a problem. You never saw him in any dress other than plus fours, stockings and brogue shoes. Every back end he would set out at the bottom of the village with 2 butter baskets full of apples. He had quite an orchard and he would call at every cottage offering apples free of charge, as many as you liked until his baskets were empty. Then back to Winton House to refill his baskets and start off again where he had broken off. He kept going until he had been round all the village. He was also keen on photography and painting; and also a keen naturalist. The Highlands of Scotland being his favourite haunt. Wilf Bousfield, his next door farmer neighbour, would accompany him as driver and companion.

Winton Common

The Common consisted of first the pun fold, then 2 ponds, and if very wet these two ponds merged into one. Two rubbish tips which had been two sandstone quarries, I presume from the enclosure days. Everything imaginable was tipped in the tips. Most things now collectors pieces. Bottles, tins, cycle parts, old buckets, bed ends, etc. There was no refuse collection by the council as of today but nearly house with a family had a bogie - a wooden soap box on 2 pram wheels plus 2 wooden shafts. was the main transport up to the tips. As everybody had coal or log fires all the ashes were saved for earth toilet purposes.

Transport

As regards the rail network, Kirkby Stephen played a major part with Kirkby Stephen East being the junction linking the Eden Valley to Carlisle. Over the top to Darlington and down to Tebay and Lancashire and West Cumberland. And it also was a Loco depot with its own sheds and maintenance staff and nearly every goods train going over the top had to have a 'banker' engine to Stainmore Summit and this the LNER line handled a lot of traffic consisting of coke trains from the east coast for the iron foundries of West Cumberland and pig iron back to the East Coast. With the LMS from Leeds to Carlisle also coming through Kirkby Stephen West down Mallerstang and then the Eden valley to Carlisle, so Kirkby Stephen was a large hub in the Northern railway's network. All livestock wagons when required made up the passenger trains plus they also had a large guards van which was available for all agricultural produce. If you had a sheepdog sold to Mr. X twenty miles away, it went in the guards van. After paying its carriage and it being correctly labelled, Mr. X person, X station, etc., and the same with calves which had to be correctly bagged so they were in a semi sitting up position. And crates of rabbits and hens, milk churns, bicycles; any commodity the railways could handle it. Every day you could hear when any train loads of stone or lime were leaving Hartley quarries to go over the top. With an engine at each end the train reversed out of the quarry and with the engines keeping control down the line to Kirkby Stephen until the 35 - 40 truck train was clear of the quarry. and then the pressure and fun started. From going down an incline to going up the incline. The front engine in theory was pulling the front half and the back engine pushing the other half, but with a lot of wheel slipping, screaming wheels and whistle blowing, plus jets of steam and smoke, it often seemed some time before the train was mobile. We often for curiosity checked how many was being pulled and how many pushed. As they got going past as we worked in the adjoining fields. Therefore LNER Kirkby Stephen in the 30s was just as big if not bigger an employer as the quarries and farming.

Greengrocers

I can only remember 2, one was Mr. Johnson with his model T Ford van with side curtains. One side fruit and veg and the other side fresh fish. His grandson still has the Model T Ford van, registration number EC34 and the other greengrocer was Dog Tom, with his pony and flat cart. Dog Tom always prided himself on a smart horse and cart turn out. There could have been others which I can't remember.

Garages

Kirkby Stephen had in those days quite a reputation. At one end you were Hooked and the other Dunning. Arthur Hook was the first coming in from the Winton end and he not only sold petrol, but specialised in re-bores and later in diesel injectors. Your car in those days was not a car of any consideration unless it had had at least two or three re-bores and oversized pistons and new big and little ends fitted. Only the influential used petrol. Those trying to run a car or motorbike not so well off always mixed so much paraffin to eke out the petrol. Petrol at 1s or 5p was considered very expensive. The next garage, North Road Garage, Hardy Johnstones, all the locals knew Hardy as 'Colossal'. It was an expression often used by Hardy. Red Lion Garage was the next which also ran a taxi service. Opposite the King's Arms. Ken Sayer was the proprietor of the Red Lion Garage. American Buick cars were Ken's specials and how many he used to pack in to take parties to Askrigg, Hawes, Lunds, Sedbergh, South Stainmore, Great Musgrave and Sandford dances, was anyone's guess. The Kirkby Stephen Gaiety Dance Band had a good following, with Mabel Braithwaite on the piano, Walter Fox 'Foxy' on the cornet, Ossie Bradbury 'Strauss' on the saxophone, and Gerald Holmes 'Geraldo' on the drums.

Also another feature of Great Musgrave Sandford dances was Jimmy Dent from Brough, with Jimmy over loaded, his was quite a turn, doing a waltz, embracing a chair as a partner.

Then there was the central garage at the Union Square. Finally Dunnings, opposite Grey Gables.

Tradesmen

Every Spring the Odd Bobs Sods man used to appear; with his pins, needles, safety pins, cottons, threads, thimbles, laces and other small haberdashery. He carried all his wares in a square box which was waterproofed with a light type of lino and it had a broad strap which went round the back of his neck and when he lifted the lid up, samples of all his wares were displayed on the underside of the lid. Pins were sold in dozens and they were threaded through a stiff pink paper, 12 pins across. Depending how many dozen you required, he just cut x strips off. He just seemed to appear and called on every house and was civil and tidy, then disappeared again.

Always around Appleby Fair and Brough Hill Fair time you had the gypsy ladies selling their wares, mostly clothes pegs, hand made blankets, lucky sprigs of white heather, etc. They stood out a mile with their jet black hair, beads and shawls. If you didn't buy from them they would go down your path chittering away, putting all sorts of curses on you. At the same time of year there was the knife sharpening man with his big wheel which he trundled around and the tin Smith, 'Any pans to mend?' was another, but these characters seemed to fade away before the war. Tin was the basic metal for nearly all household accessories. Tin mugs, kettles, pans, plates, dishes, buckets, milk cans, etc. Every household had a supply of easy fitted tin washers and bolts and nuts for simple repairs. But saved the larger repair jobs for the travelling tin smith. Now enamelled, glazed earthenware, Pyrex, and plastic have taken over.

Kirkby Stephen Tradesmen

It seemed to be a status relating to local tradesmen that after they had seen their shops opened up and things going all right, that they went along to their regular barber for a shave and a bit of crack. The lather boys made them ready and well lathered for the barber with his cut throat razor. You weren't right popular if you went in for a haircut before nine o'clock.

Kirkby Stephen Livestock Dealers

Reference to the local KS livestock dealers, there were others, but namely, Jack Chapman at Levens House 'Dealer Jack'. Len Bousfield Senior, Gorton House, 'Popsha Len'. Jack Chapman, Holme Farm, 'Lion Jack'. The two Marston brothers, Crogling Castle, John and Willy. Willy was also a butcher by trade. The sheep dealers, Jack Ellwood, Winton Field, and his brother, Alf, Row End, Warcop. The Udales of Ornside. Willy Pratt the calf dealer and there were others. It seemed to be an occupation many tried. Some more successful than others and every village seemed to have one with a flair for dealing.

Another Kirkby Stephen activity now defunct was the gas works. The man who was not only the manager, but did all the work entailed, stoker, coke extractor, keeping the gas pressure right, abstracting the coal tar, and any fitting jobs in the town, he was the jack of all trades. 'Mr. Sykes'. In winter when demand was at its highest he had one or two regular roadies who did so much manual shovel work in exchange for somewhere dry and warm to sleep and a meal. His wife was very helpful as a lot of his trade to non gas users was coke and gas tar. Most sales of coke would be in 4 stone lots, take your own hessian bag, shovel your own into the skip on his weighing machine and she would check for correct weight. Pay cash and off you went, walking home with the coke over your bicycle cross bar. And when broken down into small pieces, it was a good cheap supplement to coal. As regards the gas tar, many farms and cottagers used gas tar to preserve their outbuildings, doors, gates, henhouses, etc. It gave them a bright black looking finish and it was said if you never missed a year the gas tar in time held the doors, gates, henhouses together. Here again you took your own tin or bucket and it was sold by the gallon. If you called for coke and he was clean out he would tell you the next abstraction was in half an hour. you could keep warm and wait, then watching him abstract the coke into a quite big metal two wheeled barrow and when full, he would take it outside and tip near his weighing scales and then he would give you the job of hosing it down until cool enough to bag. Every time you went into Kirkby Stephen you always glanced to see whether the gasometer was low, half full or full. Another use made of the gas house was its weighbridge, for cartloads of different crops etc. as the only other weighbridges were at the other end of town at the stations.

Kirkby Stephen Auction

On every sale day before selling began, the auctioneer would go into the centre of the sale ring and first of all he would ask somebody to draw the ballot and the number drawn was the first animal to be sold. your draw in the ballot if lucky to be in the middle of the sale could be beneficial. After the ballot was announced, the auctioneer gave the bell rope to someone to give a few good pulls and after this the auction commenced. On the farm sales on the farm it was customary for the person selling up to provide everyone attending the sale with a knife and fork cold meal, but due to the war it had to be discontinued. It was the same as after funerals. There was always a funeral tea for all present and it was jokingly known who were the professional attenders. Another aspect of a farm sale was to obtain the runner job for the auctioneer. This was to stay close to the auctioneer whether he was selling in the yard or field and as his clerk completed a sheet with x sales details he then handed it to you t take into the sale office which was generally in the farm kitchen and the going rate irrespective of what the size of sale was always 2 bob/10p which us lads considered 'money for old rope'. As for getting stock to the auction which was all on foot or by train, groups of farmers used to join up generally on the village green, maybe 5 or 6 different owners with say 12 animals or more but with 5 or 6 persons you had better control over your stock to the market. Providing there were at least a couple of you gailylish and if you had hit a bad trade it was the same procedure taking them back home. The only difference was that they beat you home, they knew the way better than you.

Farming Details

In autumn you only had to have 1 hard frost and you were in business bagging leaves as after the frost the biggest proportion of leaves fell and it was an after school job and the farmer used them for bedding in the byres to help to keep the cows clean. And for better cleaning out. They were never dry enough for young calves bedding.

Village Life

Every night after 1933, when Express Dairies first opened up at Appleby, those who had started to supply them had to take their milk to Kirkby Stephen Low Station for transit by rail to Appleby. The only 2 I can remember were Wharton Steel, Prospect Farm and Lance Metcalfe, Howgill Farm and they took turns nightly but as it became the norm for the new and more reliable way of income from farming it was not long before lorry collection took over ex the farms direct to Appleby.

Otters on the Eden

To set the ball rolling, I give my memories of the last time I saw an otter hunt on the upper reaches. Perhaps someone has a more up-to-date version, but my version would be 1936/7. How far up the river they had come, I wouldn't know, but we could hear the hounds baying into Winton Village from somewhere near Beck-A-Waden, so off we ran and on arrival the hounds had an otter holed up. Using underwater tree roots to keep the hounds at bay about 150yds up the river from where the Winton Beck joins the River Eden, these larger trees on the Bank were just under the steep edge and on the field above joining the Main Road was then a Larch Plantation. Well after some time with the huntsmen and helpers who had both ends of the River where it broadened and was shallower watching that the otter didn't escape up or down the River.

After some time the otter made a dash across the river and made it to the opposite bank before the hounds caught it and that was the last time I saw the otter hounds round the Kirkby Stephen area.

One other connection with otters came to light in 1962/3. Lunesdale Farmers for a new depot purchased Jack Sowerby's scrap yard and part of G Bousfields, Old Fountain Farm, adjoining field, to build a new warehouse depot and at the time of writing it is now the Co-op Superstore, and when coming to lay drains they dug through good red soil for 3 to 4 ft and then encountered a solid layer of limestone and in this limestone they came across a 12" to 18" fissure, so to test it to see if it had any connection with the River Eden approx. 100 - 120 yds away 3 x 40 gallon drums were filled with water and a tracer colour dye added, and with men on the River, the 3 drums were tipped down the fissure and sure enough it arrived in the River and this outlet was then used as a top water drain. Getting back to the otter aspect, when word got round about this fissure in the rock out of the river, going under the river footpath under the field where Taylor's roundabout and fun fair used sometimes to set up then under the main road and then 20 - 30 yds into the field.

Well, more than one of the old-timers poachers/hunting men living round the bottom of Kirkby Stephen, and there was some of them, remarked, 'Well, that solves a mystery!' apparently on many previous otter hunts and if they had an otter between Eden Bridge and the Saw Mill they always lost track of the otter, so it was assumed the otters could get up the fissure and sit out the hunt.

In the later 30s bread and confectioners vans started to come round the villages and one salesman driver George or Tommy Lancaster from Penrith with his Birketts bakery van was a popular salesman. He knew all his customers and always had a good story to tell them. His most popular one was about Love bread. When asked how trade was George would remark 'In general, gailey good,' but his results from his love bread could be better. You know I have 4 spinsters in Winton on it. I supply them with specially baked love bread every week, but up to now, not much success. They try hard when it is the Chapel

Anniversary, always a new hat and dress, and they always make a note from the quarterly circuit plan of any eligible bachelors coming to preach. But I keep hoping and they keep hoping, you never know. What can I sell you today, love?'.

With respect to Fred's goats on Winton Common, we were often told that if you are going onto the common, make sure you keep away from that old billygoat or else you will be coming home stinking 'to high Heaven'. I have often wondered what a 'to High Heaven smell' was.

With respect to the different butchers coming around, one of their biggest sales amongst the working class families was 'potted meat'. Or from Porky Dowson, the pork butcher, ' brawn'. Potted meat or brawn were the equivalent of today's modern fridge for the butcher. Every night all meats getting too near to their modern term 'sell by date' were cut up small and into his set pot boiler. Boiled until tender, then well seasoned, and ladled out into enamel dishes to set. Cold ready for the next day's trade. I still enjoy potted meat when obtainable.

Ducks

Nearly every farmer kept ducks, but not only for eggs and table birds, but to combat 'yoose husk' among young calves when first turned out to grass. It was thought that in the youse life cycle snails were part of it and the ducks were always housed in or with access to the calf garth and nearby beck.

Village Life

If we had to forget to mention Albert, our forefathers would not forgive us, as Albert Loveday who resided in Hartley was the local road length man for Hartley and Winton Parishes. With his shovel and barrow, brush and clay pipe, you could use Albert as a clock. As his hours were 7.30 a.m. - 5 p.m. and if he was heading out of Winton to Hartley late afternoon, you could bet it was a quarter to 5. Every day, weather permitting, he kept all the gutters cleaned, drains clear and road side edges trimmed. When his heaps of gutterings needed moving, the local man with his horse and cart came along. It was a job keenly sought after by local farmers to get a horse, cart and man contracted to the Council for the summer months. To cart chippings to the tar sprayers, and cart water with the Council's own water cart to the steamroller and in general any other carting required. I think the going rate for carthorse and man was under 5s per day. But it was a feather in your cap if you got a contract. Very much prized was the empty tar barrels which had changed from wood to tin and which were non-returnable after use. But first of all after setting fire to them to clean them of tar then you cut the ends out and down one side and then when flattened out, you had a good sheet of tin for roofing or sides of any type of hut you cared to design. Duck, goats, hens, dogs, hay, geese and general purpose. In conjunction with used split railway sleepers, or rail bars, which you split to size required, another use of the barrels was to fire and then just cut one end out and you had a first class provin bin, kist or chest. A lot more rat proof then any wooden one. Ex railway sleepers were generally easy to come by, as all railmen received x number of sleepers per annum, as part of their wages.

Anthony Allen - Mickey Mouse

Well, where Mickey Mouse came from, I wouldn't know, but she was an all black cow with a white face and black ears and hornless. The first Friesian/Hereford cross to be seen in the District and she stood out among all the shorthorns and she became a village character. In summer Anthony Allen's cows went up through the village in the morning and back down in the evening. Mickey Mouse was the boss cow, always in the lead. If you stood in the middle of the road, she would come up to you, have a sniff or a lick then walk around you. She was very much part of Winton and she must have been around 4 or 5 years.

Re 3 ploughing farms - Winton Manor, Windy Gate and South View

Another feature re working horses was to see the horse man when carting to or from land some distance away operating with 2 horses and carts. When on the road he walked just behind the wheel of his first cart and controlled that horse with long reins, the 2nd horse by rope shank. But these horses didn't take long to learn about double carting and maybe at times kept the horseman right.

Village Sports

Some of the main activities at local sports 'quite a variety':

For ponies: straight knock out jumping by raising the bar. Straight gallop x times round the track, varying is distance with height of pony. Walk trot and gallop - generally one lap walking, one lap trotting and one lap galloping. Plus various horse and rider competitions, many now seen at the Pony Show, Wembley.

For the Trotters: various distances, but as the trotters' form was supposed to be known they were handicapped from scratch to x seconds start as it was always a saddle trot, sulkys still unheard of.

For the athletes: 100 yds sprint to fell race, pillow fighting, pole jumping.

Motor Cycles: Junior and Senior scrambles, plus distance races x times around the track

In the 30s a motorbike was the first step for anyone in mechanised transport in the village and it was the farmer or his son or the elder single established hired man who had one. There were some super models of that era. Hand gear change, carbide lamps, telescopic forks unheard of and from 250cc to 1,000cc, but mostly in the 250 - 350 range. Petrol 1s a gallon, and still too dear. A drop of neat petrol, straight into the carb to get started and then your mixture of petrol and paraffin took over and you knew every bike which was on the mix by all the backfiring it was doing. Famous makes were BSAs (Birmingham Small Arms), AJS (All Jerks and Stops), Matchless, Francis Barnett, Brough Superiors, Ariel; and the Yankee imports, Harley Davidsons and Indians. The AA patrolmen and the Milk Marketing Board's recorders in their infancy had motorbikes and box side cars, plus any business who could afford a bike plus box to carry men or materials about was deemed to be doing all right.

As for sport, the three local lads for local sports or Newcastle and Middlesbrough cinder tracks were Walter Fox 'Foxy' of Stainmore, Johnson Ingham of Brough, and Dougie Chapman of Crosby Garrett. If you had not been to Bainbridge motor bike sports, you hadn't seen 'owt.

Hound Trailing: Senior trails and puppy trails.

Something for everyone. Finishing time - darkness.

Quoits

Every Spring it was the start of the quoiting season and we knew at Winton when Waugh lads of Winton Hall and Cleasby lads, Burns House re-dug the pits, renewing the clay and making sure the ringer peg was dead centre and on a good fine night by 8 o'clock there could be 20 or more players and spectators. Nearly all other villages had a quoiting match on their local sports days. Generally a straight knockout. 1s entry fee, winner take all. Plenty of venues had 20 or 30 shillings to be won. As Winton was a full length pitch with adult quoits, you had to be pretty mature to handle them.

Whose Dog?

Now every now and then a stray dog from another village or outlying farm would be slatching around a certain village farm, hoping to do a bit of courting. The hired lads soon had their eyes on it. 'A potential tinning job'. So getting to know it, quietly until they caught it and then the word was out - they are tinning tonight. So we were all there on the square and somebody produced a small tin, no lid, with a hole through it for a piece of string. The string was attached to the dog's tail. Upon the dog being released, what a rattle. That was the last time you saw that dog in your village. It was said that one farmer turning out one morning, saw his dog looking very sorry for himself, still with tin attached, remarked to the dog, 'That'll learn thee. It is better than any twice telling thee'.

Ratting

Some winter nights when all the hired lads, farmer's sons and us younger lads had congregated on the village square, the hired lads would say, 'How about a night ratting? The moon is just right'. They decided who was going and to which farm. So if you were counted as going, it was home for a stout stick, then off you went and by that time of night the rats were on their favourite feeding grounds. Generally meal houses or pigstys. So many of you were flushers out, and the rest spaced on the outside. A good bag was 10 or 12 but if you only managed a duck, it had been a disaster. Joseph Coward at Manor House Farm was the vermin paymaster. For every rat's tail, but they must have been caught in Winton Parish, he paid 1d per tail. Where he produced his money from, may have been a levy on the rates.

Our Postmen and their bicycles

The regular postman for Winton was Joe Steadman and for Hartley, Frank Thornton. 6 days a week, year in, year out, whatever the weather. Joe would leave Kirkby Stephen by 7 a.m. and all houses and farms to Winton then Winton Village, then Kaber village, then all the holdings right up South Stainmore to Summit Cottages. He would then wait at Summit Cottages until a certain time and then return collecting from the Summit, South Stainmore, Kaber and Winton boxes. Frank would leave at the same time, starting at Hartley Village, all farms to Ladthwaite, then to Rookby, Heggerscale, and Belah Cottages, with all the holdings in between. Then, leaving his bicycle, he had a 4 mile walk, Oak Bank, New Hall, Stow Gill, Wrenside, High and Low Ewbanks, then collecting from all boxes - Belah Cottages, Heggerscale, Rookby and Hartley. These two posties were very much part of the local community. You could nearly set your watch by their regular times.

Strong of the arm, but weak in the head

Well, what does the above mean to a young lad just starting out on farm work? You see, nearly every farm job had an easy or a hard way to do it. If you didn't learn the correct way and went bull necked at it, you were classed as above. But the boss or gaffer, or older fellow workers, saw that if you were making hard work of it, they would readily explain to you or illustrate to you the correct way. As you were the next main mechanical unit, after the horse on the farm, it paid you to learn all you could. The two main items on the farm that you handled most, were hay and manure. But as both were to be handled loose, it was all hard work. In hay time, one job that could give you some hard graft was having to fork off a load of hay which had been loaded slap happy. For easy forking, you had to be able to follow the correct loaders pattern and the laid down pattern was first fill your cart kist to be level with your shelvings, then starting with your two back corners, and then your locking piece in the centre of them continue doing this until you were to the front of your kist. Then the front corners and next your centre locking piece and the pattern again for all future rounds. When forking off you follow the same pattern in reverse order. The difference in being able to follow the pattern in reverse order and the difference in being able to follow the pattern as against trying to get a forkful just anywhere, you could hardly credit it - what a difference! Another factor when forking to the loader is that all forkfuls must be of equal size and this is a knack you learn depending how thick your row of hay is. On larger farms the same man would load all the carts and another doing all the forking off and if possible, the same two men forking on.. So all knowing each others styles, it made the job a lot easier. On carting manure, you loaded your cart in wedges, the depth of the kist, starting across the front, continue doing the same to the neck and to unload, do it in the reverse order. You could go on, it doesn't matter what farm job you had to do, it paid to watch the old farm hands and take notice. There is an old saying, 'A day you haven't learned anything, is a day lost and wasted'.

Religion

Winton, as all other upper Eden villages, was very strong in supporting the Chapels, Churches and the Temperance Movement. In Winton there were two Chapels: High Chapel being the Baptist, and the Low Chapel, better known as 'Up the Steps', the Methodist. The school was used once per month for the Church Service in conjunction with Kirkby Stephen Church. The top Chapel was where the Sunday School was and it was automatic for all children to attend as soon as they could walk. Mary Waugh, Winton Hall, and Albert Strong, Orchard House Farm, were the two main teachers, with others helping as well. The Reverend Collis, was the Minister in charge and our main contact with him was when we were practising for the Anniversary. He was nearly always brought in to lay down the law, as it was really a pressgang job to say a piece both at the afternoon and evening services. In winter when it was cold we always made for 'Up the Steps'. It was not such a big chapel, but nice and warm and at the evening service it nearly always finished with a prayer meeting. There were some very strong preachers and one used to look at us and with gusto used to say, 'If he only had yar foot in the vineyard,' and another was always on about, casting out his net, 'what a catch, what a catch'. But it was the Chapels who made our only treat; some years a day trip to Morecambe on Walton's bus, and some years, if funds were not so good, a picnic tea and sports day in the field going down to Mosscroft and there was always the Band of Hope demonstration, one year at Kirkby Stephen and the next at Appleby.

School

The only other treat other than from the Chapel was from the school. As on the Thursday afternoon before Good Friday, one of the school managers used to come in and every pupil received a large jaffa orange and a coloured paste egg on behalf of the managers. Joe Coward of J and M Coward, Manor House Farm, was generally the Manager concerned. But as he went on to marry Miss Kent, the Head Teacher, he was killing two birds with one stone.

Blacksmiths shops

Although the Blacksmiths were always busy shoeing roadworking horses there were many horses on the hill farms which were never shod at all. Very rarely doing any road work, their feet were always trimmed when necessary. Another job for the local half-veterinary handyman. Every village had one, whether it was castrating, hoof trimming, bull ringing, butchering and cutting up of pigs and sheep. Cow ruling or horse docking. John Coward at Winton was the first call when any of these required doing in the village and Billy Coulthard was always on call but his area was more out of the village.

Kirkby Stephen

I may be wrong but the first dustcart I can remember for North Westmoreland District Council was Joe Furness with his piebald horse and block cart on ex wagon axles with rubber tyres. With bow shafts and extra deep sideboards, always both carthorse and cart and Joe immaculate with broad rimmed trilby. Joe was a bit of a showman attending the local shows etc. whenever there were any jumping classes. Him and W J Dent were keen rivals. But they made the show and he also farmed Holme Farm and the official local rubbish tip for

Kirkby Stephen was on the road to Smardale. First up Wiseber Hill and then right for Ravenstonedale and right again for Smardale His cart plate was North Westmoreland Rural District Council.

Joey Forster or Foster, Kirkby Stephen

Joey Forster or Foster was the farm man for George Bousfield, Old Fountain Farm, and Joey was always known as Swervy Joe due to his ability that having delivered milk from the two cans hanging from his sit up and beg bike and finishing up near the low station he returned down to the old fountain in style with it being all down hill he used to get a bit of speed on any person or vehicle in the way he swerved round them, slalom skiing fashion. In the 30s before Express Dairies came onto stream, there were 6 or 7 milk retailers in Kirkby Stephen and Hartley. Competition was very keen with morning and evening deliveries.

Domestic water - lead piping

You were often told by our seniors that if you are going to drink from a tap always make sure you run the tap first, before extracting your drinking water as the water pipes would be nearly certain to be made of lead and any lead sediment or other sediment would have gathered up next to the tap and there were farms whose water was extracted from where there were old lead workings.

General farming; snow broth

Every winter, maybe only once, or perhaps 3 or 4 times, that after a heavy fall of snow and then a thaw, the beck would run high due to all the snow melting. A lot of white froth would appear in any slack or back eddies. This was called snow broth and as all cattle used the beck for their water requirements they nearly all got what was termed black 'watter'. The snow broth made their dung very loose and black just for a day or so, but the farmers used to welcome them having black 'watter' as they always seemed to thrive better after it.

Mowd and Lime

What was the road like from say Kaber Cross to Beck A Waden? Well, it was sunk at least 4 to 5 feet below field level and a right snow trap and in winter people just used anybody's fields to get around the blocked parts. Snow cutting had to be done by hand. Farm men, if they were free between bullocking for 4 or 5 hours, could sign on with the local surveyor at 1s per hour and as they couldn't get on with any field work, it was a good idea. Well, the first improvement was rounding the square corners to round corners, both at the bottom road ends and the winds end. But the road was still narrow with passing places. So the next scheme was to widen it, piece by piece. On the opposite side to the village there was at least 4' of soil to dig out as all fields on that side all had steep clicks up into them from the road level. In those days you could have as much good soil as you wanted as long as it was a handy tip as near as possible to the excavation. Well M and J Coward, Manor House, and J. Marston, South View who had ample space on their side of Lady Ing Lane from Winds End to the Cow Pasture Gate, approximately 150 yards and 12' wide, the biggest heap of topsoil us kids had ever seen. In the years that followed, every year they mixed a portion with cob lime just at the falling stage and then carted it out and set out manure wise to be hand spread. What value this mixture had! Manor House and South View was good land in good heart. I wouldn't know, but they must have thought it had some. Similarly every 3 or 4 years the mud was cleaned out of the local ponds and mixed with lime to form a type of fertilizer. Winton Parish had its share of lime kilns for lime burning.

General farming; 3 musts:

You weren't classed as a farmer or farm worker unless you had a wire nail, often a used one, and a length or two of binder twine (Mikel) in your pocket. With these you could mend a fence or gate until they could be repaired later. A hessian sack was a must if the weather was showery. It was thought that if you kept your shoulders dry, that was it. The sack around your shoulders and fastened with a nail under the chin was your first number 1 protection.

I think I have given a fair description of how things ticked over, but not in correct rotation, in the 30s. In how everyone lived around Winton, Hartley and Kirkby Stephen area, the farming community and my own memories. Norman Tebbit told us all in the early 90s to 'Get on your bike'. It was certainly 'Get on your bike' in the 30s. I hope you have enjoyed 'Just a North Westmoreland Lad'. I could keep on writing more, but for your benefit, 'Enough is Enough'.

Mowd and Lime

What was the road like from say Kaber Cross to Beck A Waden? Well, it was sunk at least 4 to 5 feet below field level and a right snow trap and in winter people just used anybody's fields to get around the blocked parts. Snow cutting had to be done by hand. Farm men, if they were free between bullocking for 4 or 5 hours, could sign on with the local surveyor at 1s per hour and as they couldn't get on with any field work, it was a good idea. Well, the first improvement was rounding the square corners to round corners, both at the bottom road ends and the winds end. But the road was still narrow with passing places. So the next scheme was to widen it, piece by piece. On the opposite side to the village there was at least 4' of soil to dig out as all fields on that side all had steep clicks up into them from the road level. In those days you could have as much good soil as you wanted as long as it was a handy tip as near as possible to the excavation. Well M and J Coward, Manor House, and J. Marston, South View who had ample space on their side of Lady Ing Lane from Winds End to the Cow Pasture Gate, approximately 150 yards and 12' wide, the biggest heap of topsoil us kids had ever seen. In the years that followed, every year they mixed a portion with cob lime just at the falling stage and then carted it out and set out manure wise to be hand spread. What value this mixture had! Manor House and South View was good land in good heart. I wouldn't know, but they must have thought it had some. Similarly every 3 or 4 years the mud was cleaned out of the local ponds and mixed with lime to form a type of fertilizer. Winton Parish had its share of lime kilns for lime burning.

General farming; 3 musts:

You weren't classed as a farmer or farm worker unless you had a wire nail, often a used one, and a length or two of binder twine (Mikel) in your pocket. With these you could mend a fence or gate until they could be repaired later. A hessian sack was a must if the weather was showery. It was thought that if you kept your shoulders dry, that was it. The sack around your shoulders and fastened with a nail under the chin was your first number 1 protection.

I think I have given a fair description of how things ticked over, but not in correct rotation, in the 30s. In how everyone lived around Winton, Hartley and Kirkby Stephen area, the farming community and my own memories. Norman Tebbit told us all in the early 90s to 'Get on your bike'. It was certainly 'Get on your bike' in the 30s. I hope you have enjoyed 'Just a North Westmoreland Lad'. I could keep on writing more, but for your benefit, 'Enough is Enough'.